Cultural Life

in the Federal Republic of Germany

Inter Nationes Bonn

Cover picture
Bonn's Bundeskunsthalle after a design by Austrian architect Gustav Peichl. It was opened on 19 June 1992 with five exhibitions. *Title picture:* sculpture (detail) by French artist Niki de Saint Phalle, with view of one of the Hall's three light towers. (Photograph: Klaus Stahl)

Editorial Revision: Detlev Moos, Thomas Piltz and Stefan Elsberger

Translation: Patricia Crampton and Robert C. Flood

Typesetting, Printing and Binding: Passavia Druckerei GmbH Passau

© 1993 by BMS Platt GmbH, Munich
in collaboration with Inter Nationes, Bonn

Printed in the Federal Republic of Germany

Contents

A.R. Penck, "Standart VI", 1983, 350 × 260 cm, Museum Ludwig, Cologne: The Dresden artist Ralf Winkler chose the pseudonym "A.R. Penck" to conceal his participation in exhibitions in West Germany from the authorities of the former GDR. In 1980 he was able to emigrate to the Federal Republic.

Preface

Cultural life in the Federal Republic of Germany, with its multiplicity and inherent contradictions and controversies, has its roots in centuries of German tradition. Moreover, cultural events and developments in Germany are part of European culture.

The creative power and imagination which impart so many and varied impulses to the cultural life of our country are especially favoured by three factors.

Freedom of art, science, research and teaching is guaranteed as a basic right by the Constitution. Besides this legally secured opportunity for development, there are the material opportunities. The protection of copyright, organized in a way which is financially relatively satisfactory, a broad and diverse system of publishing, concerts, galleries and museums as well as numerous state and private promotion programmes, allow many artists to devote themselves fully to cultural creation. A third factor which has a positive effect on a versatile cultural life is education. Numerous private and state schools or colleges of music, art, film, and other artistic disciplines provide sound training and creative stimulus for the rising generation. Apart from some Federal prizes and promotion programmes, together with its foreign cultural policy, the Federal government maintains a low profile in the sphere of cultural policy.

Pursuing the tradition of an independent cultural life, cultural policy is left in the hands of the Federal *Länder,* but they too have delegated the major part of their tasks to the communities, in which cultural life as such proceeds. This kind of polycentric cultural work and experience had already developed in the Middle Ages in large and small provincial capitals, in the principal secular and ecclesiastical seats, in free cities and commercial centres. Though some centralization occurred with the foundation of the Empire in 1871, the member states which continued to exist largely retained their independence in the cultural field.

This did not change until the years 1933 to 1945. Regulations regarding content, prohibitions, and politically-motivated spoon-feeding by the National Socialists in almost every area of cultural life, combined with anti-creative bigotry, inflicted severe wounds on cultural development in Germany and did lasting damage to Germany's cultural standing abroad. Many artists died or emigrated, large numbers of works of art were destroyed.

Goethe's line from Faust: "Rivers and brooks are freed from the ice by the fair, life-giving glance of spring" can be applied to the development of German cultural life after 1945. Immediately after the war, in a period of great material want, actors and musicians began to work and experiment again.

The division of Germany by the victorious powers had very different effects on this "Renaissance". The record of the Potsdam Conference of 2 August 1945 certainly stated that the German people should be given the opportunity to reconstruct their life on democratic foundations; not much later, however, the Soviets were beginning to establish a communist system with a planned economy in their occupation zone. The introduction of different currency systems in East and West and the failure of the attempt to create a unified government for Germany led ultimately, in 1949, to the founding of the FRG (Federal Republic of Germany) and the GDR (German Democratic Republic). Their social systems not only exhibited serious theoretical differences; the practical organization of their political, administrative, economic and cultural structures developed on widely divergent lines.

In the West a federalist state arose, with pluralism, parliamentary democracy, the rule of law, transparency and the chance of free cultural evolution. In the East all the powers of the state were in the hands of the SED (Socialist United Party of Germany). Government, People's Chamber, the judiciary and the administration simply fulfilled the wishes of the Party. Civil freedoms – freedom of opinion, freedom of association, freedom of the Press, freedom to travel – appeared in the Constitution but did not exist in practice. Opponents were persecuted, millions of citizens were spied on by the state security service. The arts too – the fine arts, literature, the theatre – and the artists themselves were subject to state control and censorship. In the Federal Republic of Germany, on the other hand, cultural life was free to evolve and develop naturally from the start, supported not only by the free democratic system, but also by economic prosperity.

Following the dissolution of the GDR as a state and the unification of Germany on 3 October 1990, the five newly formed federal *Länder* of Saxony, Saxony-Anhalt, Thuringia, Brandenburg and Mecklenburg-Western Pomerania largely adopted the system and laws of the former Federal Republic. This meant that in the new federal *Länder* culture, its institutions and representatives, artists and academics, were released from the constraints of their former dependence on the state for all decision-making.

By now the Association of German Writers, founded in the former Federal Republic, has its local groups of authors in the new federal *Länder* as well, the museums and theatres receive no official instructions as to their exhibitions and performances, and publishers compete on the open market without supervision or censorship, as in the old Federal Republic. Though some problems still exist in certain areas with regard to the transition from the previous spoon-feeding by the state to free, responsible organization, this is in the nature of cultural activity, and of course, of the difficulty of economic adjustment.

It is of course impossible to do justice to the cultural developments of more than forty years, and to do so to suit every taste, in such a brief survey as this. Besides the objective description of individual phenomena, the reader will also find personal opinions and assessments by the authors, which may sometimes provoke opposition. This is only natural in view of the cultural variety represented; at the same time it provides more incentives for dialogue with groups abroad interested in cultural developments, which INTER NATIONES wishes to intensify.

It is not the aim of this brochure to create or replace a work of reference. The object of this publication is to move the reader, to awaken his interest, and ultimately to give pleasure by providing information through a combination of words and pictures.

Bonn, Summer 1992

Dieter W. Benecke

The Herzog August Library in Wolfenbüttel (Lower Saxony), which now houses some 700,000 volumes, is one of the most famous libraries in the Federal Republic of Germany (above). Author and philosopher of the Enlightenment Gotthold Ephraim Lessing (1729–81) worked as librarian here from 1769 until his death.

The World Museum for the Art of Printing in Mainz recalls the beginnings of book culture: here a demonstration of the printing process in memory of Johannes Gutenberg from Mainz, who invented letterpress printing with moveable types in 1450.

Literature

On 4 July 1945, barely two months after the end of World War Two, German intellectuals met in the Berlin "Radio House" to found a "Cultural Association" which, as its full name indicated, was intended to promote the "democratic renewal of Germany". The writers returning from exile (Bertolt Brecht, Johannes R. Becher, Anna Seghers, Arnold Zweig) or who were finally able to give up their "inner emigration" (Ricarda Huch, Gottfried Benn, Werner Bergengruen), wanted to gather together the anti-Fascist intellectuals: they founded the journal *Aufbau,* the weekly paper *Der Sonntag,* as well as the Aufbau publishing house. In 1945 no one believed that the division of Germany would last very long. The first congress of German writers in October 1947 was a pan-German occasion. Yet four weeks later the "Cold War" was a German reality: in the American and French sectors of Berlin the "Cultural Association" (93,000 members) was banned.

There was never a "zero point" for German literature. Hans Carossa, Ernst and Friedrich Georg Jünger and Ernst Wiechert had continued to write in the Germany of the "Third Reich", Hermann Broch, Alfred Döblin and Thomas Mann brought significant works back from their exile – and the need, the hunger for books was equally great in all the occupation zones of Germany.

The new German literature arising in the first post-war years took stock. It spoke of the "literature of the ruins", of the "literature of total destruction". Radio and theatre plays by Wolfgang Borchert (*The Man Outside,* 1947), short stories by Heinrich Böll (*The Train Was on Time,* 1949; *Traveller, if You Come to Spa …,* 1950; Wolfdietrich Schnurre (*Die Rohrdommel ruft jeden Tag,* 1950), and above all poetry, aimed at communicating the reality of ruins and rubble, the decline of ideals and hopes, the deep traces of external and internal destruction, and making them comprehensible. The poetry of Wolfgang Weyrauch (*An die Wand geschrieben,* 1950), of Günter Eich (*Abgelegene Gehöfte,* 1948; *Untergrundbahn,* 1949), of Peter Huchel (*Gedichte,* 1948), of Karl Krolow (*Gedichte,* 1948; *Heimsuchung,* 1948) – authors who had begun with nature poetry during the National Socialist regime – were much read, quoted and learned by heart in those years. Immediately after the Second World War many German people looked to literature for help in life's problems.

Post-war literature was crystallized in literary-political journals *(Aufbau,*

Frankfurter Hefte, Merkur, Der Monat, Das goldene Tor, Ost und West, Sinn und Form, Der Ruf) and in "Group 47", which was founded by Hans Werner Richter. Until 1967 "Group 47" brought together authors, critics and publishers who listened to readings from new texts, criticized and discussed them and awarded a prize for the best unpublished work. In the period when literature and politics stood furthest apart, in the 1950s of the German restoration, "Group 47" was more than a loose association of people from the Federal Republic who were interested in literature: "Group 47" articulated the political demands of literature and by means of appeals, manifestoes and open letters, gained respect as a moral opposition. At the same time it encouraged the internationalization of German post-war literature, a development which found visible expression in 1972, when the Nobel Prize was awarded to Heinrich Böll.

In the Soviet zone of occupation, in the young German Democratic Republic, the SED assumed the role of a state party and even by September 1948 those who governed cultural policy in that party were asking: "Have we produced works in the last three years which reflect the mighty process of peaceful democratic reconstruction? ... The great novel of reconstruction has not yet been written, the life of its builders not yet given artistic form." In the GDR it was decided to publish a mass edition of a "library of German progressive writers" in the spring of 1949; at the same time a "national prize" was funded for "outstanding achievements by German scholars, artists, writers, engineers, agronomists, technologists, master craftsmen and workers", in three classes (25,000/50,000/100,000 marks). In that same spring of 1949, however, the first cultural policy campaign began in the Soviet zone of occupation, the "East Zone": it condemned "formalism and decadence" and supported "realism". Those attacked included: the painter Karl Hofer, former vice-president of the "Cultural Association", but also Picasso, Dali, Thornton Wilder, as well as the editors of the "Cultural Association" paper *Der Sonntag* – the latter because of objectivist tendencies. Writers were exhorted with increasing intensity towards the Stalinist variant of realism, "socialist realism". The statute of the Soviet Writers' Association, which was recognized as exemplary, defined this "ism" in the following words: "Socialist realism ... demands of the artist the truthful and historically concrete account of reality in its revolutionary development. The truthfulness and historical objectivity of the artistic depiction of reality must be combined with the task of changing and educating the workers in the spirit of socialism ..."

The literature of the fifties in the Federal Republic reacted to the political, economic and social restoration: to rearmament, the accession to NATO, the "economic miracle". The authors confronted the heritage (including the literary heritage) of National Socialism and tried to oppose the reinforced old powers with a democratic attitude. With the currency reform, interest in literature as an "aid to life" had declined sharply in the western zones. The dramatists, and with them the theatres, were restrained with regard to German subjects in the fifties. The programmes of those years featured mainly plays by foreign writers (T. S. Eliot, Thornton Wilder, Eugène Ionesco, Albert Camus, Jean-Paul Sartre), and contemporary German-language drama was written in Switzerland by Friedrich Dürrenmatt (*The Visit*, 1956; *The Physicists*, 1962) and Max Frisch (*Andorra*, 1961). The dual task of reappraising the past and criticizing the present was most clearly assumed by the novel. Especially in the novels of Alfred Andersch (*Flight to Afar*, 1957; *The Redhead*, 1960), Heinrich Böll (*And Where Were You, Adam?* 1951; *The Unguarded House*, 1954; *Billiards at Half Past Nine*, 1959), and Günter Grass (*Tin Drum*, 1959), the reflections of Nazi-past and Economic-Miracle-present are interwoven. The poetry of the 50s exhibits two characteristic tendencies. While Gottfried Benn, with his phrase "das Gegenglück, der Geist" ("the counter-fortune, the mind"), propagated a form of withdrawal from contemporary reality, and Paul Celan, in his "hermetic poems" (*Mohn und Gedächtnis*, 1952; *Sprachgitter*, 1959), formulated the experiences of National Socialism, the poems of Hans Magnus Enzensberger in particular (*Verteidigung der Wölfe*, 1957; *Landessprache*, 1960) are poetic contentions with political issues. Günter Eich gave important impulses to the radio play of that time, especially with his radio play *Träume* (1953). Eich found a way, suitable for the media, of establishing a (nightmare) world through language, by which means he created a tradition for many authors such as Ingeborg Bachmann, Wolfgang Hildesheimer, and Walter Jens. The experimental radio play of the 60s was aimed above all at the dissolution of conventional speech patterns and modes of perception. The most important authors here are Jürgen Becker, Ludwig Harig, Helmut Heissenbüttel, Dieter Kühn, and Franz Mon.

In the GDR, literary works were increasingly appearing in the fifties which were later to be referred to under the key words reconstruction, production, business and agricultural novels. These books depicted land reform, the distribution of great estates among refugees and agricultural workers or the reconstruction of a business. All of them contained one or two good people, with the Party Secretary on their side, against one or two bad people: big farmers, bourgeois scientists, covert Western agents. At the end good prevails with the good people: socialism is at hand. In 1951 the eagerly awaited first production novel of the GDR appeared: Eduard Claudius, *Menschen an unserer Seite*. Its hero, the Hoffmann kiln mason Garbe, who prematurely dismantles the still heated kilns and thus becomes an "activist", also later became a subject for Bertolt Brecht and Heiner Müller. Brecht's working of Maxim Gorky's *The Mother*, his libretto for Paul Dessau's opera *The Trial of Lucullus* and his arrangement of Lenz's *The Bailiff* were regarded as "formalistic" and "decadent". The GDR poets, and above all Johannes R. Becher, first Minister of Culture of the GDR, concocted poems mainly on the basis of a type of folk song exhortation and praise of the Soviet Union. Only Bertolt Brecht's stern philosophical occasional poems (*Buckow Elegies,* 1953) showed qualities of thought and set a style. GDR cultural policy resisted the influence of the Moderns but also of Expressionism and the proletarian literature of the twenties and gave absolute form to the literary aesthetic of, for instance, Georg Lukács.

In April 1959, after a preliminary anti-revisionist campaign, the SED once again made attempts to bring the authors round with the help of the grass roots. At an authors' conference in the Bitterfeld chemical complex the later so-called "Bitterfeld way" was brought into being under the motto "Take up your pens, comrades, socialist national culture needs you!" Workers were to write, authors were to work in the factories. The results of the authors' work visits and the circle of writing workers which arose thereafter were worthy, but in terms of literature almost entirely valueless. The greatest influence was exerted by Christa Wolf's story *Der geteilte Himmel* (The Divided Heaven) 1963, partly based on the author's experiences in a freight car factory. Peter Hacks' impressive factory drama *Die Sorgen und die Macht* was taken off because it was allegedly "not sufficiently future-oriented". Karl-Heinz Jakobs' *Beschreibung eines Sommers* (1961), Erwin Strittmatter's *Ole Bienkopp* (1963), Erik Neutsch's *Die Spur der Steine* (1964) appeared in large editions, but in the case of these novels the heroes gave offence: Jakobs' Tom Breitsprecher was said to be acting immorally because he consorted with the wife of a colleague, Strittmatter's Ole Bienkopp was ahead of his time because he established an agricultural cooperative, and moreover, his death was inexplicable. Erik Neutsch was said to have allowed a party secretary to act immorally because although married, the man had made a woman engineer pregnant and then abandoned her. In the GDR literature of the fifties and early sixties the desire for completely "exemplary" heroes was still detectable.

Literature in the Federal Republic in the sixties, the years of the declining Economic Miracle, of the Great Coalition and the Extra-Parliamentary Opposition, bears the stamp of far-reaching politicization which functionalizes poetry: literature is meant to serve the political struggle. The poetry of, for instance, F.C. Delius (*Wir Unternehmer,* 1966), Erich Fried (*und Vietnam und,* 1966; *Zeitfragen,* 1968), and Yaak Karsunke (*reden und ausreden,* 1969) therefore equally focuses on the subjects of the class struggle and exploitation, student rebellion and the Vietnam war, as do the political songs of Franz Josef Degenhardt, Hanns Dieter Hüsch, and Dieter Süverkrüp. German-language drama takes historical and contemporary topics as subjects –

often in the form of documentary theatre: Rolf Hochhuth (*The Representative*, 1963; *Soldiers*, 1967), Heinar Kipphardt (*In the Matter of J. Robert Oppenheimer*, 1964), Günter Grass (*Plebeians Rehearse the Uprising*, 1966; *Uptight*, 1969), Peter Weiss (*The Investigation*, 1965; *Discourse on Vietnam*, 1968), and finally Hans Magnus Enzensberger (*Das Verhör von Habana*, 1970). It is not major politics but oppressive everyday reality that is brought to the stage by authors following the tradition of social criticism in the dialectal popular play. The principal figures of the plays of Martin Sperr (*Jagdszenen aus Niederbayern*, 1966) and Franz Xaver Kroetz (*Wildwechsel*, 1971; *Stallerhof*, 1972) are often outsiders in a village community, driven to ruin by the narrowness and narrow-mindedness of their surroundings. Although the novel as an extended epic form was not directly suited to political activism, nevertheless the important novelists of the 60s were political authors. Especially Heinrich Böll (*The Clown*, 1963; *The End of a Mission*, 1966; *Group Portrait with Lady*, 1971), Günter Grass (*Dog Years*, 1963; *Local Anaesthetic*, 1969; *From the Diary of a Snail*, 1972), Martin Walser (*Halbzeit*, 1969; *The Unicorn*, 1964; *Der Sturz*, 1973; *Jenseits der Liebe*, 1976), and Siegfried Lenz (*German Lesson*, 1968; *Das Vorbild*, 1973; *Heimatmuseum*, 1978) exemplify the type of writer for whom literature and politics, social experience and aesthetic composition are closely linked. The entirely realistic novels increasingly focus on present-day conflicts and problems in the Federal Republic of Germany as their themes; Uwe Johnson, on the other hand, dealt with the partition of Germany (*Speculations about Jakob*, 1959; *Third Book About Achim*, 1961; *Two Views*, 1965). Authors of the Dortmund "Group 61" such as Max von der Grün (*Irrlicht und Feuer*, 1963; *Stellenweise Glatteis*, 1973), Erika Runge (*Bottroper Protokolle*, 1968) or Günter Wallraf (*Wir brauchen dich*, 1966; *13 unerwünschte Reportagen*, 1969; *Der Aufmacher*, 1977), and of the "Study Group on Literature of the Working World", proceeding from this in 1969, pursued political goals by literary means. Their aim was to analyze the world of industrial work and its social problems by means of literature. At the same time, literature is intended here to serve the forming of political consciousness among writers; this is literature by workers and literature for workers in one. The key-word "descriptive literature" covers authors who do not so much interpret social reality as try to represent it (apparently) without emotion. These include above all Jürgen Becker (*Felder*, 1964; *Ränder*, 1968), Rolf Dieter Brinkmann (*Keiner weiss mehr*, 1968), Alexander Kluge (*Lebensläufe*, 1962; *Schlachtbeschreibung*, 1964), and Dieter Wellershoff (*Ein schöner Tag*, 1966; *Die Schattengrenze*, 1969). Cutting across these trends at right angles, we find "concrete poetry" (Helmut Heissenbüttel, Ernst Jandl, Ferdinand Kriwet, Franz Mon, and others), which tries to ignore all abstract meaning-content of linguistic communication, to do away with traditions of form, and to proceed from the material character of language: language becomes the object of literature.

The 1960s not only brought about the politicization of literature, they gave new self-confidence to the writers. The authors announced the "end of modesty" (Heinrich Böll) and in 1969 founded the German Authors' Association, which in 1973 joined the Printing and Paper Trade Union and merged in 1989 with other associations in the Media Trade Union. This unionist orientation was to help to push through the demands for old age provisions specific to the profession, for the removal of the "school book paragraph" allowing free reprints, and for a library lending fee in favour of the author, as well as for an improvement of publishing contracts.

The centrally controlled literature of the GDR developed in the second half of the sixties quite differently from the literature of the Federal Republic: the majority of authors believed that they could improve the political system; they had missed the experiences of the youth revolts in the western countries, they were largely excluded from the world-wide debate on the relationship between literature and politics. In the opinion of its leaders, the GDR was destined, on the "Bitterfeld Way" to become the literary paragon of the socialist camp. In 1965 at the 11th plenary session of the Central Congress of the SED, those politicians responsible for culture and the writers obedient to them accused the insubordinate authors of "nihilism" and "scepticism". Werner Bräunig (thanks to a realistic chapter of a novel on the German-Soviet Wismut AG), Stefan Heym (because of his play *Die Langeweile von Minsk,* which was not published in the GDR), Wolf Biermann (for his songs and poems), Peter Hacks (for the land reform play *Moritz Tassau*), Heiner Müller (for the production play *Der Bau*) and many others became the targets of considerable criticism. In the so-called poetry debate, which began in the summer of 1966, auhors and critics did in fact avoid direct complaints against the cultural policy of their country but debated new literary qualities. Adolf Endler and Karl Mickel, both famous poets themselves, were able in 1966 to publish an anthology of GDR poetry under the title *In diesem besseren Land* (In this better land). Official criticism failed to find in this volume the authors it regarded as important, while readers were astonished at the wealth spread out before them and previously almost completely withheld from them by GDR publishers. This new poetry of the GDR was "subjective" and intended in this way to intervene in the construction of socialism.

The debate on the "poetry of the second stage of assimilation" was conducted in the columns of the FDJ (Free German Youth) student newspaper *Forum* in particular. This brought the names of Heinz Czechowski, Rainer and Sarah Kirsch, Volker Braun und Günter Kunert to the attention of many readers for the first time.

The new critical, subjective GDR poetry was also respected abroad. There had already been an awareness there that following the "literature of recon-struction", with the so-called "literature of completion", novels and stories had been produced in the GDR which aimed at fulfilling higher literary demands than before. Among others, Brigitte Reimann's story *Die Geschwi-ster* (1963), Jurek Becker's novel *Jakob der Lügner* (1968), Hermann Kant's novel *Die Aula* (1964) had attracted attention, but so had the novels, stories and poems of Johannes Bobrowski (*Levins Mühle,* 1964; *Litauische Claviere,* 1966), the prose of Franz Fühmann (*Das Judenauto,* 1962; *König Ödipus,* 1966; *Der Jongleur im Kino oder die Insel der Träume,* 1970), the plays of Peter Hacks (*Margarete in Aix,* 1966; *Amphitryon,* 1967), Heiner Müller (*Philoktet,* 1968; *Ödipus Tyrann,* 1977), Volker Braun (*Die Kipper,* 1962). The literature of the authors who were now concerned with everyday life in the GDR, the literature which illuminated the present day in the light of past ages, made a not insignificant contribution to gaining international recognition for the GDR as a state. The authors' next step was in connection with the rejection of objectivity, the striving for expanded subjectivity, au-tonomy. Fritz Rudolf Fries told the story of two intelligent young East Ger-mans who know how to live (*Der Weg nach Oobliadooh,* 1966); Christa Wolf coined the phrase "subjective authenticity", telling the story of the life of a disappointed GDR woman (*Nachdenken über Christa T.,* 1968) or of the tensions in a GDR family (*Juninachmittag,* 1967); Alfred Wehm, one of the many writer/teachers in the GDR, appealed for a school which took the individual seriously (*Pause für Wanzka oder Die Reise nach Descansar,* 1968). Fritz Rudolf Fries's book was not allowed to appear in the GDR until 1989 and Christa Wolf's *Nachdenken über Christa T.* was published be-latedly and in a reduced edition.

In the Federal Republic the journal *Kursbuch,* published by Hans Magnus Enzensberger, had announced in 1968 the "death of literature" – it did not contribute to the resolution of social and political grievances. But in the mid-70s "fine literature" was flourishing again, produced by Austrian and by German-speaking Swiss authors as well. In the period of halted reforms and the "change of direction", it became a medium in which, though com-plex political problems were no longer handled, personal (political) experi-ences were. A number of thematic strands can be clearly distinguished. At-tention to the individual, his rediscovery as a literary subject, is particularly evident in the novel. Important authors of the post-war period produced autobiographical works: (Max Frisch: *Diaries 1966–1971,* 1972; *Montauk,* 1975; Wolfgang Koeppen: *Jugend,* 1976; Thomas Bernhard: *Die Ursache, Der Keller, Der Atem, Die Kälte,* 1975–1981; Elias Canetti: *The Tongue Set Free, The Torch in my Ear, The Play of the Eyes,* 1977–1985); the treatment of the theme of the "fathers" became a real fashion (Ruth Rehmann: *Der Mann auf der Kanzel,* 1979; Peter Härtling: *Nachgetragene Liebe;* Christoph

Meckel: *Image for Investigation;* Barbara Bronnen: *Der Vater,* all 1980) and the experiences of the student revolt (and also of terrorism) were assimilated by literature (Uwe Timm: *Heisser Sommer,* 1974; Bernward Vesper: *Die Reise,* 1977) up to and including Peter Jürgen Boock's *Abgang* (1988).

The recollection of personal individuality and the construction of a personal identity are central patterns of the women's literature arising in the 70s: Karin Struck (*Klassenliebe,* 1973; *Die Mutter,* 1975), Verena Stefan (*Häutungen,* 1975), Brigitte Schwaiger (*Why is There Salt in the Sea?,* 1977), Eva Demski (*Goldkind,* 1979). In documentary literature, self-ascertainment and political claims overlap: in Uwe Johnson's monumental *Anniversaries* (4 volumes, 1970–1983), in the panorama of the bourgeois world of Walter Kempowski (6 volumes from *Tadellöser & Wolff,* 1971, to *Herzlich Willkommen,* 1984), and in the revealing report of the absolute bestseller *Ganz unten* (1985) by Günter Wallraff.

The most popular fantasy novels were written by the children's book author (*Jim Knopf*) Michael Ende: *Momo* or the extraordinary story of the time thieves and the child who brought back stolen time (1973) and the *Neverending Story* (1979), a novel about poetry and the threat of its loss, went into millions of copies.

Trivial literature, e.g. Willi Heinrich (*Der Väter Ruhm,* 1988), Heinz G. Konsalik (*Der Arzt von Stalingrad,* 1984) and Johannes Mario Simmel (*Im Frühling singt zum letztenmal die Lerche,* 1990) gradually turned away in the eighties from the major theme of the Second World War. More popular were stories of love and hatred in exotic places or novels on environmental themes (Simmel). Individual attempts by established literary criticism to take this "new" trivial literature seriously were without success on either side. Political everyday experience is the subject of numerous works of fiction, such as the initially violently controversial story that has now become textbook reading: *The Lost Honour of Katharina Blum* (1974) by Heinrich Böll, *Die Herren des Morgengrauens* (1978) by Peter O. Chotjewitz, and also *Lenz* (1973) and … *schon bist Du ein Verfassungsfeind* (1977) by Peter Schneider.

Even more than the novel, the poetry (Jürgen Theobaldy, Wolf Wondratschek, Nicolas Born, Ulla Hahn) and drama of this period, e.g. Botho Strauss (*Trilogie des Wiedersehens,* 1976; *Big and Little,* 1978; *Kalldewey Farce,* 1981), are characterized by the assimilation of everyday reality. Here an extraordinary sensitivity to psychological processes generally goes hand in hand with the precisely detailed description of banal everyday life.

The retracing of the life of an individual artist, supported by documentary evidence (Peter Härtling: *Hölderlin,* 1976; Wolfgang Hildesheimer: *Mozart,* 1977; Dieter Kühn: *Ich, Wolkenstein,* 1977) ultimately belongs to the rediscovery of the literary subject as referred to above: a "psychologism critical of the age" (Marcel Reich-Ranicki) is thus as a whole a basic feature of literature after the "death of literature".

An echo of the discussion of '68 about the status of literature is provided by the polemical controversy over the more recent works by Botho Strauss (*The Young Man: A Novel*, 1984; *Diese Erinnerung an einen, der nur einen Tag zu Gast war*, 1985) and the Austrian Peter Handke (*Der Chinese des Schmerzes*, 1983; *Repetition*, 1986). In the radical rejection of social functionalism ("One writes solely to serve literature", Botho Strauss) some see nothing but "neo-theological vacuity" (Helmut Heissenbüttel), and others the sole opportunity for "Poesie" (*sic*) to survive in this world contaminated by the mass media.

In the GDR many authors became aware in the seventies that they were not really needed in the construction of socialism – Wolf Biermann, who constantly wanted to "get involved" through songs, poems and plays, was first punished by a ban on publication and performance and then, in 1976, exiled. The protest of the leading authors in the country against Biermann's exile was of course a signal: from then on the writers practised the propagation of hidden truths, without conforming at the same time to "real socialism" – or they left the country. Stefan Heym (*Der König David Bericht*, 1972), Ulrich Plenzdorf (*Die neuen Leiden des jungen W.*, 1972), Franz Fühmann (*22 Tage oder Die Hälfte des Lebens*, 1973), Volker Braun (*Unvollendete Geschichte*, 1975), Reiner Kunze (*Die wunderbaren Jahre*, 1976), Günter de Bruyn (*Märkische Forschungen*, 1978) criticized the GDR and its spy system, its fear of jeans, its efforts to dismiss fascism as having been "rooted out", its inability to understand the young people's longings for freedom. Among many others, the following left the GDR: Günter Kunert, Sarah Kirsch, Reiner Kunze, Hans Joachim Schädlich, Karl-Heinz Jakobs, Bernd Jentzsch. The literature of reconstruction, of completion, of development, was followed in the GDR by a literature of crisis. With increasingly modern narrative methods and with the help of a radical imagination, the GDR authors developed negative, warning utopian themes – for instance, Irmtraud Morgner (*Leben und Abenteuer der Trobadora Beatriz*, 1974), Werner Heiduczek (*Tod am Meer*, 1977), Helga Schütz (*Julia oder Erziehung zum Chorgesang*, 1980), and Christa Wolf (*Kassandra*, 1983). At the same time, women's literature arose in the GDR, prose documenting the reality of the promised emancipation, e.g. Maxie Wander (*Guten Morgen, du Schöne*, 1977), or the fictitiously accused, as in Brigitte Reimann's *Franziska Linkerhand*, 1974, or Gerti Tetzner's *Karen W.*, 1974. A third reaction of GDR literature in the seventies was attached to the return of suppressed, covert, everyday fascism. Erich Loest has a man who wants to turn his daughter forcibly into a high performance swimmer, sworn at as "you goddamned Fascist". (*Es geht seinen Gang ...*, 1978); Christa Wolf recalls how the first

generation of the FDJ (Free German Youth) emerged from the last generation of the BDM (League of German Girlhood) (*Kindheitsmuster,* 1976);
Stephan Hermlin described the terrors of the struggle in exile and warned
against regarding themselves as "victors of history" (*Abendlicht,* 1979);
Heiner Müller sketched mythical images of history for the Nazi years, for
the GDR years (*Germania Tod in Berlin,* 1971; *Die Schlacht,* 1975), for the
world as a whole (*Macbeth,* 1971; *Hamletmaschine,* 1977).

The literature of the eighties in the Federal Republic makes use, as one of
its contemporary critics puts it, of the "cipher of the body" (Hubert
Winkler): in the prose of Anne Duden (*Das Judasschaf,* 1985), Bodo
Kirchhoff (*Infanta,* 1990), Reinald Goetz (*Irre,* 1983; *Kontrolliert,* 1988)
there appeared "variously structured texts, in which the image and concept
of the body could assume widely differing positions". However, it is undoubtedly true that many authors write songs of farewell, farewell to the
days when literature supported sense and practicality: Botho Strauss
(*Fragmente der Undeutlichkeit,* 1989; *Kongress. Die Kette der Demütigun-
gen,* 1988), Peter Handke (*Versuch über die Jukebox,* 1990), Christoph
Ransmayr (*The Last World,* 1988) and Brigitte Kronauer (*Berittener
Bogenschütze,* 1986; *Die Frau in den Kissen,* 1990) seek explanations, old
myths, memories, in our daily lives, in Spanish hotels, in the footsteps of
Ovid or Joseph Conrad.

The literature of the eighties in the GDR reveals that socialist realism is
dead. Its place has been taken by all those contents, forms and methods of
thinking, seeing and writing known to the literature of the Federal Republic
– the literature of the GDR has "caught up" with the Federal Republic, it
too communicates the "damaged life", the "suppressed individual" (Heinrich
Mohr), the "relationship between self-determination and collective demands,
of adaptation and resistance" (Lothar Jegensdorf). "The literature of the
GDR is entering into its experimental epoch", wrote Wolfgang Emmerich
in 1989 on the GDR literature of the eighties. While the older people saw
themselves as being in a "railway carriage", which was the "steam engine
of history", with which they believed they had to travel "to the interior"
(Volker Braun), the younger people, those "born into" the GDR (Uwe
Kolbe), had long run away from this "railway carriage": the GDR had "never
interested" them (Sascha Anderson). The young GDR authors of the eighties, officially scarcely recognized, had communicated with and acknowledged each other through readings organized by themselves, through
painters/poets books, and through underground papers: they were looking
for the explosive force of the present in the art of language, and rejected
"enlightened" attitudes and historical thinking. The outstanding representatives of the older generation wrote "warning literature" increasingly in the
eighties (Hans Mayer), in which they recorded the life of the eighties in

terms of socialist realism: careerists in Günter de Bruyn (*Neue Herrlichkeit,* 1984), conformist, hardened contemporaries in Christoph Hein (*Der fremde Freund/Drachenblut,* 1982), the contrasts between ruler and ruled in Volker Braun (*Hinze-Kunze-Roman,* 1985), the real life of the proletariat in Wolfgang Hilbig (*Die Weiber,* 1987); *Alte Abdeckerei,* 1991).

With the collapse of the Wall and the restoration of German unity, German literature might also be able to enter a new phase. A first attempt by critics of the old Federal Republic of Germany simply to declare the literature of the GDR obsolete, out of date, provincial and superfluous had some effect. In particular, the authors of the GDR were accused of having stabilized the social system of their state, and being privileged and paid for it. In reality many authors had been fighting for the independence of literature, almost all of them offering help in the problems of life. Only a relatively small number were working for party and state. The central administration of the book trade and publishing in the Ministry of Culture approved the printing of the books and thus functioned as a censorship authority. At no time were there salaries for authors in the GDR – there was, however, a carefully graded system of reward and punishment, in the shape of privileges and promotion measures. The GDR Writers' Association served the interests of authors as well as their attachment to the state order. The view that the literary history of the GDR would have to be "re-written" in view of some spectacular *Stasi* spy cases (Anderson, Schedlinski, Novak, Kahlau), seems, when one looks at the totality of GDR literature over four decades, rather misleading. We shall see how the authors of the former GDR will write in future, but we shall also see that the new political and social conditions will leave their mark on the future literature of the united Federal Republic of Germany.

The book as the medium of the mind also has a substantial economic dimension – though it is difficult to back this up with up-to-date figures from the reunited Germany, in view of the rapid changes taking place as the former GDR publishing houses adjust to the market economy. So we will quote some figures from the last year of the divided Germany, 1989. At that time, some 3,000 publishers in the Federal Republic of Germany issued or re-issued a total of 65,980 titles; a further 470,000 were available from stocks (in the GDR 6,093 titles from 68 publishers). This put the Federal Republic in third position in the world rankings, behind the Soviet Union and actually ahead of the USA. In the Western part of Germany 3,612 bookshops were concerned with supplying literature, in the East 1,300 bookshops – yet despite the availability, statistics reveal that in the "old" Federal *Länder* six per cent of all households still did not possess a single book …

Those who cannot or will not buy books may borrow them: in 1989 the citizens of the Federal Republic could select their reading from up to 259 million volumes in nearly 13,000 public and 5,605 academic libraries. In the last days of the GDR 110 million volumes were at the disposal of the citizens in some 32,000 public and academic libraries. Since unification the number of libraries and of units of stock and the frequency of their use has fallen appreciably in the new *Länder*.

Günther Fetzer/Konrad Franke

Important German authors from the period between the wars: from left to right: Thomas Mann (1875–1955), Alfred Döblin (1878–1957), Heinrich Mann (1871–1950), Gottfried Benn (1886–1956), Bertolt Brecht (1898–1956), Carl Zuckmayer (1896–1977), Erich Kästner (1899–1974).

Annual meeting of the German PEN-Centre from 5 to 7 May, 1988 in Bamberg (Bavaria). From Martin Gregor-Dellin, who had died on 23 June 1988, Honorary President Walter Jens temporarily took over the chair.

Elias Canetti, born in 1905 to Spanish-Jewish parents in Bulgaria, received the Nobel Prize for Literature in 1981 (on the right, the Swedish King Carl Gustav at the award ceremony); the German-speaking author's books are now published by Carl-Hanser-Verlag in Munich.

The German Library in Frankfurt/Main, the central collecting agency for all German-language publications and itself publisher of the *German Bibliography,* also opens its well-stocked archives to the public in exhibitions. The photo shows a poster for an exhibition on German literature written in exile from 1933 to 1948.

Fair buildings in Leipzig – the Exhibition Centre of the Leipzig Book Fair, which in the years of the GDR was no longer able to achieve the importance it had enjoyed in earlier centuries and also before World War Two. Nevertheless, at least while the Fair was on, reading-hungry literature enthusiasts could browse in Western books and journals which were not on sale in the GDR.

The annual grand celebration of books in Frankfurt/Main.

Number of exhibiting publishers

Year	exhibitors		
	total	German	foreign
1949	205	205	–
1950	460	360	100
1951	602	412	190
1952	857	484	373
1953	989	484	505
1954	1058	524	534
1955	1158	547	611
1956	1355	573	782
1957	1384	647	737
1958	1485	678	807
1959	1837	710	1127
1960	1904	682	1222
1961	1893	717	1176
1962	2128	719	1409
1963	2181	750	1431
1964	2274	768	1506
1965	2394	792	1602
1966	2539	819	1720
1967	2871	858	2013
1968	3048	890	2158
1969	3212	871	2341
1970	3398	855	2543
1971	3562	889	2673
1972	3719	869	2850
1973	3837	952	2885
1974	3903	952	2951
1975	4039	954	3085
1976	3946	1039	2907
1977	4534	1114	3420
1978	5098	1260	3838
1979	5045	1311	3734
1980	5302	1416	3886
1981	5534	1465	4069
1982	5688	1519	4169
1983	5890	1616	4274
1984	6169	1755	4414
1985	6635	1827	4808
1986	7005	1919	5086
1987	7191	1981	5210
1988	7965	2106	5859
1989	8189	2128	6061
1990	8492	2268	6224
1991	8417	2236	6181

Founded in the same year as the Federal Republic of Germany, namely 1949, the post-war Frankfurt Book Fairs have from the very beginning succeeded in enjoying the interest also of eminent political figures. Above: the then Federal President Theodor Heuss (1884–1963) during a visit to the Fair in 1955; below: former Federal Chancellor Konrad Adenauer (1876–1967) presents the first volume of his memoirs at the Book Fair in 1965.

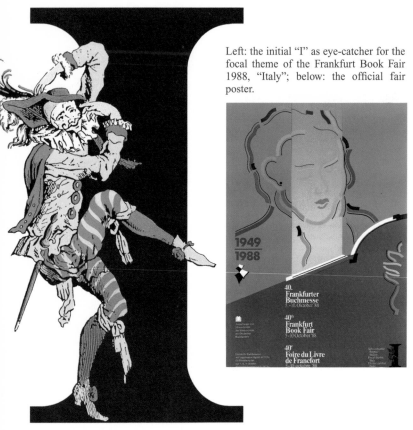

Left: the initial "I" as eye-catcher for the focal theme of the Frankfurt Book Fair 1988, "Italy"; below: the official fair poster.

The tradition of book fairs in Germany stretches back to the time of the invention of printing: the first book fairs took place in Frankfurt and Leipzig as early as in the 15th century, with Leipzig winning the upper hand from the early 18th century onward. After the interrruption due to the Second World War, the Frankfurt Book Fair, reestablished in 1949 and taking place annually at the beginning of October, is now the largest book-trade event in the world in terms of the number of titles displayed and of countries and publishers participating (cf. table on preceding page).

In addition to the literary and feature sections of the daily and weekly papers, other ▶ important intermediaries between authors and reading public are the cultural journals, which appear monthly or quarterly, and literary annuals. As representative of many titles, the illustrations show: *Text + Kritik,* edition text + kritik, Munich; *Schreibheft,* Rigidon-Verlag, Essen; *Litfass,* Piper-Verlag, Munich; *Freibeuter* and *Tintenfisch,* both Verlag Klaus Wagenbach, Berlin; *Merkur,* Verlag Klett-Cotta, Stuttgart; *Sinn und Form,* Rütten & Loening, Berlin; *Weimarer Beiträge,* Aufbau-Verlag, Berlin; *Akzente,* Carl-Hanser-Verlag, Munich.

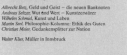

Important contemporary German women writers; from left to right: Luise Rinser (b. 1911), Christa Wolf (b. 1929), Ingeborg Drewitz (1923–86), Gabriele Wohmann (b. 1932), Karin Struck (b. 1947), Irmtraud Morgner (1933 to 1990), Sarah Kirsch (b. 1935), Maxie Wander (1933–77).

Important contemporary German writers; from left to right: Karl Krolow (b. 1915), Günter Eich (1907 to 1972), Arno Schmidt (1914–79), Stefan Heym (b. 1913), Günter Grass (b. 1927), Heinrich Böll (1917 to 1985), Siegfried Lenz (b. 1926), Christoph Hein (b. 1944).

Volker Braun
Texte
in zeitlicher Folge
Band 4

Unvollendete Geschichte
Gegen die
symmetrische Welt
Tinka
Schmitten
Notate

mdv

Siegfried
Lenz
Deutsch-
stunde
Roman

Hoffmann und Campe

Walter
Kempowski
Tadellöser
& Wolff
Roman

Max von
der Grün
Stellenweise
Glatteis

Roman
Luchterhand

STEPHAN HERMLIN
ABENDLICHT

Grass

Die
Blechtrommel

Roman

Stefan Heym
Auf Sand
gebaut

Sieben Geschichten aus der unmittelbaren
Vergangenheit

C. Bertelsmann

Heinrich Böll
Frauen vor
Flußlandschaft
ROMAN
KIEPENHEUER
& WITSCH

»Wir drängten denen, die eine
feste Hoffnung brauchten,
nicht unser Wissen auf, daß wir
verloren waren.
Doch unsre Heiterkeit, die
niemals ihren dunklen
Untergrund verlor, war nicht
erzwungen.«

Christa Wolf
Kassandra Erzählung
   und Voraussetzungen einer
Erzählung: Kassandra
Luchterhand Bibliothek

Illustration is of particular importance to books for children and young people. An example is shown from Marit Kaldhol's *Goodbye Rune,* published by Verlag Ellermann, Munich, and winner of the German Children's Book Prize in 1988. The illustrations are by Wenche Øyen, Norway.

◄ Major book titles of recent decades.

A network of children's libraries as well as children's book exhibitions and reading competitions ensures that the book tradition does not die even in the age of television. Above: a mobile library issuing books.

One of the most important collections of German literature is the Central Library of German Classics in Weimar. The photograph shows the historic library, the organization of which goes back to Goethe himself.

The "Staatsbibliothek Preussischer Kulturbesitz" in Berlin was built in accordance with the plans of architect Hans Scharoun (1893–1972). On the right, the northern staircase to the reading rooms; below, the overall view from the north-west.

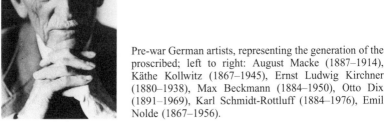

Pre-war German artists, representing the generation of the proscribed; left to right: August Macke (1887–1914), Käthe Kollwitz (1867–1945), Ernst Ludwig Kirchner (1880–1938), Max Beckmann (1884–1950), Otto Dix (1891–1969), Karl Schmidt-Rottluff (1884–1976), Emil Nolde (1867–1956).

Fine Arts

The resumption of artistic life in Germany after the Second World War can be dated back to August 1945: on 2 August Gerd Rosen opened the first gallery in post-war Germany, then still under occupation, on the Berlin Kurfürstendamm; on 5 August, five hundred kilometres to the south, the first art exhibition opened under extremely difficult circumstances in Prien, Upper Bavaria. Contemporary reports express a hunger for cultural experience which is scarcely conceivable today – and that experience was at first primarily one of intellectual freedom regained.

"Resumption" refers initially above all to the continuation of those artistic traditions, especially those of expressionism, surrealism and the ideas of the "Bauhaus", which had been interrupted in National Socialist Germany. There was very little information available about the developments that had been taking place abroad. Artists of the older or middle generation such as painters Karl Schmidt-Rottluff, Erich Heckel, Willi Baumeister, Ernst Wilhelm Nay, Fritz Winter, Richard Oelze, wood-cut artist HAP Grieshaber and sculptor Hans Uhlmann, conveyed – some of them as teachers at the academies that were re-opening one by one – the principles on which the younger artists built. Soon, however, the art of painting, especially abstract painting, that was now developing freely, met with opposition, as triggered in 1947 by the exhibition "Extreme Painting" in Augsburg. The public's tolerance and understanding of art had been unable to develop, especially in the generation which grew up in the "Third Reich", that is the younger people – the damning phrase "degenerate art" lingered in many minds and came readily to hand. In this situation, in Munich in 1949, a number of artists, including the painters Baumeister, Winter, Rupprecht Geiger, and the sculptor Brigitte Meier-Denninghoff formed the "Group of Non-Representationals", which took the name "Zen 49". "Based on the tradition of the *Blauer Reiter*", according to Geiger, "the aim of this group is to disseminate abstract art through words and pictures so that it becomes common property, that is, the decisive testimony of our time".

Elsewhere too, artists formed groups – the group "The Young West", which held its first exhibition in Recklinghausen in 1948, deserves particular mention. The artists at the core of the group were painters Gustav Deppe, Thomas Grochowiak, Emil Schumacher, Heinrich Siepmann, Hans Werdehausen, and the sculptor Ernst Hermanns. Franz Grosse-Perdekamp,

initiator of the group, wrote on its aims: "They are concerned with incorporating the technicized age, which has not yet become living intellectual
property to us, into our lives ... The young artists are ruthlessly serious
about this new reality, to which they belong in place and time, and it will
have to be observed that this art, described rather inappropriately as abstract,
is closer to reality than the so-called realistic art, which is no longer in
control of a reality which is only partially open to visual experience." Young
art in industrially oriented West Germany began in a different social environment and with different problems from young art in South Germany,
where the matter in hand was "to reduce the mysterious currents of nature
that now characterize the world-view, to an allegorical formula" (Geiger).
Undoubtedly the attention which turned to the technical and industrial reality at an early stage in West Germany helped to prepare the ground for the
particular liveliness of the artistic developments and activities that followed
there.

The living and working conditions of artists living in East Germany were
different again, since a quite differently structured artistic life developed
there from a comparable point of departure. Whereas the "cultural struggle"
in divided Berlin in the early post-war years represents a completely peaceful dialogue with the opposite position – the visitors to the Galerie Rosen
included both Soviet officers and Karl Hofer, one of the most important
cultural revivalists of that time, but also Marxists such as the philosopher
Wolfgang Harich and the architect of the Stalin-Allee, Hermann
Henselmann – yet the currency reform, the blockade and the foundation of
the two part-states within Germany, the Federal Republic and the GDR, led
by 1948/49 at latest to a split in the art scene, which has not been finally
overcome even following the collapse of the Wall and reunification in 1990.
The first "General German Art Exhibition" took place in the late summer
of 1946 in Dresden, organized by Hans Grundig and Will Grohmann. For
the first time works by Barlach, Baumeister, Beckmann, Feininger,
Felixmüller, Grosz, Heckel, Kirchner, Klee, Kokoschka and Käthe Kollwitz
could be seen again in Germany. Yet the reaction of the public was largely
one of rejection – the emotive formulae absorbed during the National Socialist period had too dominant an influence. In the autumn of the same year
the Saxon Artists' Congress in Dresden announced that a licence had been
issued for the journal *bildende kunst,* published by Karl Hofer and Oskar
Nerlinger. Its advisers included teachers from the (West) Berlin College of
Fine Arts and artists from the Soviet zone of occupation. In the Artists'
Congresses of 1947/48 which took place in other *Länder* of the Soviet zone,
however, political pressures became evident, exercised by the Soviet cultural
officers participating. Appealing to the decrees of the Central Committee of
the Communist Party of the Soviet Union on "problems of contemporary

Soviet art" they insisted on a concept of realism orientated towards naturalist principles and affirmation. In Dresden the group "Das Ufer" was founded around Hans Grundig, Otto Griebel and Rudolf Bergander, who worked for socio-political commitment and the simple depiction of the object observed. Opposed to them was the artists' group "der ruf", with Hermann Glöckner and Edmund Kesting, which aimed more at a free investigation of reality through new painterly means. A little later, Waldemar Grzimek, Karl Erich Müller, Willi Sitte and others formed the Halle group "Die Fähre" which defended the experimental aesthetic principle and also the artists' ties with the material basis of society. The question as to whether, how and in what way art functionalizes and can be included in the "class struggle", determines from then on, in dogmatic and less dogmatic phases, the art history of the Soviet zone and the subsequent GDR.

The leitmotif of the confrontation in artistic policy became "socialist realism", which was set against the horrors of a decadent western "formalism". In the "Formalism Campaign" of 1951 there were attacks on the Academy of Arts of the GDR, which tolerated "modernists" and "subjectivists" in its ranks, including such figures as Carl Crodel, a teacher at the Burg Giebichenstein College of Art at Halle, or the East Berliners Horst Strempel, Arno Mohr and Herbert Behrens-Hangeler. Horst Strempel's mural in the booking hall of Berlin's Friedrichstrasse station was whitewashed over, well-known artists and art historians (such as Fritz Löffler, the sage of Dresden art) were dismissed from their posts or forced to leave. Everything related to Expressionism – even the works of people like Käthe Kollwitz or Ernst Barlach – was acknowledged to be "profoundly dangerous" and thrust into the background until the sixties.

The "IIIrd German Art Exhibition" of the GDR in the spring of 1953 marks the culmination of this kind of self-curtailment – though it must be said in defence of the East German artists that many important painters did not take part in that exhibition, while others were rejected on the grounds of "sketchiness" or a tendency to be painterly or even abstract. At the same time, *bildende kunst* – which had long ceased to be published by Hofer and Nerlinger – was able to state in its issue 2/1953: "The coarse phenomena of formalism and other damaging, decadent art tendencies have been overcome."

From decade to decade the appearance of GDR art certainly changed: positive heroes and the romance of the tractor did not always set the tone, but the principles of political cultural control and influence, the precisely calculated system of sanctions and "promotional measures" remained. Artists like Herbert Sandberg and Willi Sitte, who had several times been disciplined in the fifties, later themselves belonged to the apparatus of power and defended the framework of thinking, directed from above, into which, however, both Picasso and the Italian *Realismo* fitted, but not Joseph Beuys and the *Arte povera*. Crusades against decadence such as the social activist exercises on the "Bitterfeld Way" haunted the artists of the GDR. The sixties brought the "Workers' Theatre" of the political illustrator Heinrich Witz and the disputes over Fritz Cremer's courageous commitment on behalf of the young generation. Leipzig artists Bernhard Heisig, Werner Tübke and Wolfgang Mattheuer provoked the viscous flow of socialist-realist deformation with a revelation of the conflicts between the individual and GDR society. They set up internal monologues as stopgaps, but also painted protests and the subjectivity of aesthetic production, against uniformity in art. The Party up to then refrained from accepting these new approaches, praising instead the cheerful illusionism of Walter Womacka, whose "Paar am Strand" later adorned school textbooks and all the dentists' waiting-rooms between Rügen and Saxony.

While the concept of realism was reduced in the Eastern part of Germany to its simplest denominator and petrified into dogma, the developments of the fifties and sixties in the Western part, the Federal Republic, led back as if in an ironic volteface of art history, to new, reflective forms of realism. At first, of course, the fifties were predominantly under the influence of the "Informal", an abstract-expressive way of painting, whose outstanding exponents were the Frankfurt "Quadriga" artists Bernhard Schultze, Karl Otto Götz, Otto Greis and Heinrich Kreuz, the Düsseldorf "Group 53" with Gerhard Hoehme and Peter Bruning, and also Emil Schumacher, Karl Fred Dahmen and K. R. H. Sonderborg. The French *"tachisme"* and the "drippings" of the American Jackson Pollock were crucial points of reference in this painting, which liberated the picture from the portrayal of reality, enabling it to become a document of the process of its creation into an existential and experiential part of reality – and it was this that opened up completely new perspectives for further development.

With the "Group Zero", founded in Düsseldorf at the turn of 1957/58 by Otto Piene and Heinz Mack, and which Günther Uecker also joined, a counter-movement came to life, which, though based on the "Informal", nevertheless turned against the latter's epigonal superficiality in a form of art which made use only of the stylistic stereotypes and not of the intellectual approach of the "Informal" artists. Light, movement, and dematerialization now became central concepts – it was now heaven, so to speak, instead of earth to which they looked; and the opportunities offered by modern technology determined the level at which artistic structuring was to take place: Piene developed his light ballet, Mack and Uecker created their rotating structures. "Zero" unfolded in close contact with artists of similar aims in other countries – Yves Klein, Tinguely, Fontana, and Manzoni among many others. Other artists who can be regarded as members of the new movement in the Federal Republic, especially Gerhard von Graevenitz in Munich, realized a stricter system of organizing the pictorial elements, in which, on the one hand, the "Informal" was once again the point of departure, as was, on the other hand, the contention with the concrete art primarily of the Swiss. With the new artistic productions, the image of the exhibition also changed, the attitude of the viewer, his participation. This change was further reinforced in the sixties by the art forms of "Happening" and "Fluxus". In the Federal Republic, Wolf Vostell and Joseph Beuys in particular worked on the development of "action art", which aimed at a unity of art and life, and they also took part in the transition to "performance art", which renounced the direct participation of the public. Beuys became the German artist undoubtedly best-known internationally today, and as teacher and thinker, one of the most important influences in the more recent art activity in the Federal Republic – especially through his reflections on an expansion of the concept of art by social and political dimensions.

With the American "Pop Art", which became known in the Federal Republic in the mid-sixties, a radical variety of realism took the floor and helped to overcome the fixation of interest on abstract art which had arisen in the meantime. A multiplicity of new figurations had already developed from the "Informal", as for instance in the works of Horst Antes. In 1955 Konrad Klapheck in Düsseldorf had already begun to counter the "Informal" with his precisely painted machines, which in a subtle way turned into manifestations of subjective ideas, fears and desires.

In different ways, Fritz Köthe, Peter Klasen, and Gerhard Richter in Düsseldorf and the painters of the "Group Zebra" in Hamburg (Dieter Asmus, Peter Nagel, Nikolaus Störtenbecker, and Dietmar Ulrich) returned to the photographic image of reality as their model. Berlin became the centre of the painters of critical realism (Peter Sorge, Wolfgang Petrick, Johannes Grützke, and others). Outside the traditional institutions, Klaus Staeck brought his critical screenprints into action right in the political arena, castigating inhuman modes of conduct with his sharp phraseology; posters and leaflets became the forms of activity appropriate to his intentions. Of special importance to the expansion of artistic activity beyond the museums and galleries was the Symposium Movement, which arose in 1959 from an initiative of the Austrian sculptor Karl Prantl. In the Federal Republic of Germany, the idea fell on particularly fertile ground: almost at once, and increasingly to this day, sculptors in particular gathered in many places to create works of art under the respective prevailing natural or urban conditions. Yet this does not affect the fact that the history of the development of fine art in the Federal Republic of Germany, seen as a succession of styles and tendencies, seems essentially to be a history of painting and its incursions into other spheres. Plastic art, to which greater attention was paid relatively late – an important date is the great sculpture exhibition of 1977 in Münster, followed in 1987 by a second major exhibition – seems to have only a small share in this history. Now, if important representatives of the plastic arts such as Norbert Kricke, Ernst Hermanns, Ulrich Rückriem, and most recently Otto Boll, cannot thus be appropriately classified stylistically and chronologically within this history, then the inference must be that the criteria of categorization are no longer appropriate to what is actually going on. The inclusion of plastic arts expands and alters the questions which must form the basis for the organization and hence the understanding of events – this is also evident in the sculpture exhibitions, when, for instance, as was the case recently in Münster, the question as to the possible functions of plastic art in the urban environment, as to the local and social context of art, supersedes the question regarding stylistic connections. And the art of painting itself undoubtedly tends towards alterations in the questions, whose reflection and fundamental formulation constitute an urgent task: for instance, the renunciation of the idea of linear progression in history is among the aspects of the neo-expressive style of painting of the "New Savages", which at the start of the 1980s dominated the art scene in the Federal Republic, and especially in Cologne (Walther Dahn, Georg Jiri Dokupil, etc.). It is demonstrated in the carefree quotation of art history, in the natural use of history as a given, freely available language to expand the concept of the present.

If, in conclusion, we take a look at developments in the last two decades of the now extinct GDR, we can observe that in spite of the repression by Party and state which continued unaltered to the end, the straitjacket of socialist realism imposed on art gradually expanded. Corners outside the official exercise of art and its spoon-feeding also opened up increasingly in the seventies and eighties. In fact, the culture of the GDR in its last years collapsed into two parts: one supported by the state, and one more or less subversive one, ranging from radical anti-art to schizophrenic forms of not-only-but-also. The possibility of refusal was, ironically enough, laid down in the system of the GDR itself: since only essentials could be bought, money played practically no role at all. In order to ensure one's existence in a world of want, it was not absolutely necessary to give in to the pressure of the Artists' Association – the development of individualists such as Gerhard Altenbourg (who exhibited covertly in West Germany even in 1964), Peter Hermann, Ralf Winkler (A.R. Penck), Peter Makolies, Peter Graf, and also Hermann Glöckner, Edmund Kesting, Willy Wolff and Carlfriedrich Claus, are evidence of this.

Despite this self-liberation in individual forms of refusal and rebellion, which had also rapidly adopted the topical vocabulary of West European art, GDR art remained largely self-referential to the end – or, to put it bluntly: a ghetto art. This aspect also determined the attention it received from "over there", from the Western part of divided Germany: here the aspect of "news from over the Wall" was always prevalent. GDR art was regarded as the evidence and seismogram of the existence, in the other part of the divided homeland, of something completely legitimate and representing an important task of art, while at the same time curtailing it in its aesthetic dimensions. The art of the former GDR must be open to the accusation that this curtailment was often easy for it to accept – and it can claim in its defence that it was never fully able to develop its true potential under the discipline of the totalitarian regime, with restricted freedom to travel and without the economic and moral support of an operative, free art market. It will be interesting to observe how experience of life in the former GDR will now be depicted, after reunification, in the work of the artists who have emerged from it and have also lost with it a part of their own identity.

Christoph Tannert

Willi Baumeister (1889–1955) developed his language of form chiefly as a result of his occupation with Cézanne, cubism, cave and African rock painting. After 1945 he also acquired great significance for the younger generation of German artists as a theorist and teacher. Shown here: "Montaru 7 a", 1953, oil on painting board, 81 × 100 cm, an example from his late picture cycles.

Rainer Fetting (b. 1949) is one of the circle of the so-called "Young Savages" whose style of painting, reminiscent of expressionism and fauvism, dominated the German art scene in the early eighties. "Downtown view", oil on canvas, 191 × 131 cm, was painted in 1987.

From painting in the Informal style, Bernhard Schultze (b. 1915) developed his informal colour sculptures, which – like "with a hand", 1966, shown here – visualize transitions from the inorganic to the organic, from human to plant life.

Horst Antes (b. 1936) developed his art figures from an Informal painting style: cephalopodes and trunkless figures like this "King" of 1967.

As artist, theorist and teacher, Joseph Beuys (1921–86) was one of the most important initiators in recent German art. Besides drawings, paintings, and sculptures, his work also includes many actions such as this one in 1972, when Beuys had himself rowed across the Rhine near Düsseldorf in an archaic dugout.

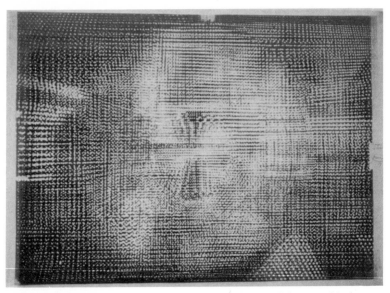

Light and movement are the decisive elements of the art of the Düsseldorf group "Zero". 1959 saw the first performance of the "Light Ballet" by Otto Piene (b. 1928), who has been director of the *Center for Advanced Visual Studies* (CAVS) in Massachusetts since 1974. Our picture shows a work of art in light-graphics produced by Piene in 1959.

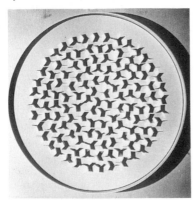

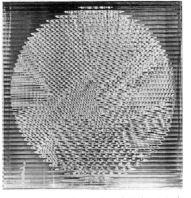

The "Kinetic Object", 1963, by Gerhard von Graevenitz (1934–83) consists of a large number of identical elements, each rotating randomly and independently on its own axis. The homogeneity of the structure is maintained in the ceaseless change.

Among the early works of Heinz Mack (b. 1931) were "light dynamoes" such as the object illustrated, dated 1960: by rotation behind corrugated glass, the structure of an aluminium relief optically takes on a flowing movement.

Art as document of the emotional state in the declining GDR: shortly before the Change in 1989, Leipzig painter Wolfgang Peuker painted the "Pariser Platz" before the Brandenburg Gate in Berlin as a no-man's land, a scene of flight and pursuit.

"Painting means shaping the picture out of paint." These words by Ernst Wilhelm Nay (1902–68) determined the path of the painter from expressionistic beginnings to a rhythmically moving picture construction of circling, floating discs of colour. "Of the Magical Yellow", oil on canvas, 162 × 130 cm, was painted in 1960.

Gerhard Richter (b. 1932) is one of the most versatile German artists of the postwar period. "Landscape with Small Bridge, Hubbelrath", 1969, oil on canvas, 120 × 150 cm, comes from the phase of artistic processing of photographs projected on to the canvas.

Strictly speaking, Dieter Krieg (b. 1937) does not paint objects – more accurately, with their help colour comes alive in a quite specific, even physically perceptible, powerful vividness. The "Fish", acrylic/oil on canvas, 160 × 315 cm, was painted in 1984/85.

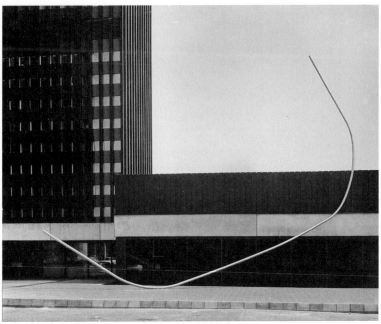

The space sculptures of Norbert Kricke (1922–84), which guide the movement of seeing towards the experience of open, unlimited space, are among the most important products of German post-war sculpture. In 1981, Kricke's "Large Space-Curve Cologne", $14 \times 17 \times 12$ m, was installed on the forecourt of the two broadcasting stations Deutschlandfunk and Deutsche Welle.

Cover pages of important art journals in the Federal Republic of Germany. The *Kunstchronik,* published by the Central Institute of Art History in Munich, has made quite a name for itself as an international forum for discussions on art history.

◄ The sculptures of Rebecca Horn (b. 1944) as, for instance, the "Mechanical Fans", aiming at the experience and expansion of physical motion, are conceived as an integral component of performances, and for some years also of filmic actions.

Emil Schumacher (b. 1912) is one of the most renowned artists of the German Informal Movement. "Barbaros" is an example of the painter's pictures, which, with
their characteristic materiality of colour, form, and destruction of form, produce an
earthy effect.

This "Albtraum" (Nightmare, 1982) by Leipzig painter Wolfgang Mattheuer (b. 1927) oscillates in the field of tension between criticism and affirmation. Mattheuer, with Werner Tübke (b. 1929) and Bernhard Heisig (b. 1925) is among the internationally best-known artists of the former GDR.

In 1955, Konrad Klapheck (b. 1935) began to paint, with the utmost precision, machines and instruments, which became as it were portraits of human feelings and modes of behaviour. Thus the typewriter, for instance, – here: "Patriarchate", 140×120 cm, 1963 – functions as a symbol of masculinity.

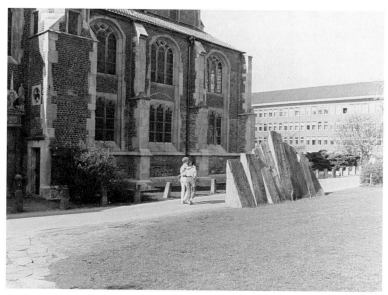

"Dolomite Cut to Size" was stone sculptor Ulrich Rückriem's (b. 1938) contribution to the great "Sculpture 77" exhibition in Münster. The wedges, which relate to the church buttresses, turn the path into a kind of alley for a certain distance.

The heroic world of labour in the GDR painting: "Der Brigadier" (Team Leader), oil, 139 × 124 cm, painted by Bernhard Heisig in 1970.

Reconstruction of the Babylonian Gate of Ishtar in the Pergamon Museum on Berlin's "Museum Island".

Museums and Exhibitions

The traditions of the German system of museums and exhibitions go back to the early 19th century. At that time state and local museums were added to the princely and ecclesiastical collections which had been in existence for quite a long time, while initiatives by the citizens led to the founding of art associations whose principal task was to organize exhibitions of contemporary art.

Historical and archaeological collections were established in addition to museums of art and art history; museums of science and technology in addition to natural history museums. Fortresses and castles were turned into show places for a large public, and following the great institutes which soon achieved world fame with their huge stocks, a large number of small museums appeared, among which collections of popular and local culture soon predominated.

Today there are rather more than 4,030 museums in the whole Federal area, about half of which are collections of popular and local interest. 44% of the approximately 3,220 museums in the eleven old Federal *Länder* are run by communities (towns), counties and districts, some 47% by associations, corporations and private companies. The proportion of museums in the possession of the Federal *Länder* amounts to about 8%. Something comparable is probably true of the five new Federal *Länder,* as soon as the responsibility for the 810 or so museums there has been decided on. The fact that only 17 museums, not even half of one percent of the total, belong to the highest organ of state, the Federation, can be explained by the federal structure of the Federal Republic of Germany. It leaves political responsibility for cultural matters to the Federal *Länder* or communes, without denying the demands for appropriate assistance when these arise, as for instance in the acquisition of works of art of national importance, or co-financing of exhibitions of comparable character.

Baden-Württemberg has the most German museums (748), followed by Bavaria (704), North Rhine-Westphalia (481), Lower Saxony (417), Hesse (362), Saxony (271), Rhineland-Palatinate (215), Thuringia (139), Saxony-Anhalt (135), Schleswig-Holstein (120), Brandenburg (116), Mecklenburg-Western Pomerania (105) and the Saarland (44), as well as the city states of Berlin (110), Hamburg (47) and Bremen (20).

Among the most important state museums are the great cultural and art

history collections in Berlin, which, having formerly been Prussian possessions, have been reunited in the "Prussian Cultural Property Foundation"
created by Federal Law. Torn apart by the consequences of the Second
World War and in particular the four decades of political division of the
capital, they now comprise 28 institutes which are gradually to be gathered
together in 17 museums. Those of world rank were the Egyptian and Pergamon Museums, the Painting Gallery of Old Masters and the National
Gallery of Modern Art. The Germanic National Museum in Nuremberg
became the most important centre for the collection of German art and
cultural history, while the German Museum in Munich occupies first place
among European museums for natural sciences and technology. Those responsible for all these institutions are foundations or public corporations
which are jointly financed by the Federation and the *Länder*. Operating on
the same basis are also the Roman-Germanic Central Museum in Mainz,
the German Mining Museum in Bochum, the German Maritime Museum in
Bremerhaven and the Natural History Research Institute and Senckenberg
Museum in Frankfurt am Main.

A few of the museums run by individual Federal *Länder* are no less important and also have an international following, such as the Bavarian State
Painting Collections with the world-famous Old and New Pinakothek, the
Glyptothek, the State Collection of Antiquities and the State Gallery of
Modern Art in Munich, the State Art Collections of Dresden with the galleries of old and new Masters and the "Green Vault" (a treasure chamber of
princely arts and crafts), the State Galleries of Stuttgart and Karlsruhe (both
in Baden-Württemberg), the North Rhine-Westphalian Collection in Düsseldorf with the finest works of the classical moderns, and the Painting Gallery
of Old Masters with the State Art Collections in Schloss Wilhelmshöhe in
Kassel (Hesse). Also worth mentioning are the Hessian Regional Museum
in Darmstadt, the Rhenish Regional Museum in Trier (Rhineland-Palatinate), the Herzog-Anton-Ulrich-Museum in Brunswick and the Regional
Museum in Hanover (both in Lower Saxony), the State Gallery Moritzburg
in Halle/Saale (Saxony-Anhalt) and the Schleswig-Holstein Regional Museum in Schleswig. The Overseas Museum in Bremen and the Hamburg
Kunsthalle with its outstanding collection of 19th century German painting
are maintained by their city states, while the art collection of the Veste
Coburg and the Regional Museums in Bonn and Münster/Westphalia are the
responsibility of regional corporations, the Coburg Regional Foundation for
the former and the Rhineland and Westphalia-Lippe Landscape Associations
for the latter.

Among the most noteworthy communal collections are the Roemer- und
Pelizaeus-Museum in Hildesheim, devoted to antiquity, the Sprengel Museum in Hanover, the Essen Folkwang Museum (merged in 1970 with the

German Poster Museum), the Von-der-Heydt-Museum in Wuppertal, the Municipal Hall of Art in Mannheim, Munich's Municipal Gallery in Lenbachhaus with its rich collection of works by the "Blauer Reiter" group of artists and the Museum of Fine Arts in Leipzig. The highest number of municipal museums, ten in number, are at present to be found in Frankfurt am Main, since the older institutes, such as the Historical Museum, the museums of arts and crafts, for ancient sculpture (Liebieghaus), for ethnology and for pre-history and ancient history have been joined by important new foundations: the German Film Museum (1980), the German Architectural Museum (1984), the Jewish Museum (1988) and the Museum of Modern Art (1991). Even so, these collections are exceeded as regards volume of stocks by the eight art and cultural history collections of the city of Cologne, including the Wallraf-Richartz-Museum of Ancient Art, the Ludwig Museum of Modern Art (focusing on pop art and the Russian avant-garde), the Museum of Applied Art and the Museum of East Asian Art. Almost all these institutions derive from foundations by citizens, in which the citizens often not only contributed their own collections but also financed the building of the first exhibition buildings. This applies to most of the German towns in which there are neither princely seats nor republican centres.

A number of public collections are maintained by the churches, including the Diocesan Museums in Cologne, Mainz and Trier. The same naturally applies to the various cathedral treasuries and other repositories of sacred cultural objects. There are quite large private museums which exist generally as bodies run by industry or as company foundations, such as the Ernst-Barlach House in Hamburg (Hermann F. Reemtsma Foundation) and the Käthe-Kollwitz-Museum of the Cologne District Savings Bank, let alone the group of museums in which the collection of historical evidence is linked with commercial interests. This applies to museums of viniculture and brewery, of pharmaceuticals, playing cards and porcelain, and certainly to the increasing number of car and engine museums. The oldest civic foundation of a museum, the "Städelsche Kunstinstitut" in Frankfurt am Main, founded in 1816, is now largely maintained by public funds in association with the Municipal Gallery. Private foundations and donations by individuals and groups do, however, continue to constitute an essential factor, if not the backbone of the financing of numerous museums whose budgets are too modest to allow them extensive acquisitions. The constantly growing number of collections all over the world and the associated escalation of prices plays a decisive role in this connection. It is quite true that well-founded and factually undisputed appeals for subsidies directed to the public legal entities in Germany seldom go unheard, but increasingly the museums count on non-public donors, who are also able to act more flexibly. These have for the most part formed themselves into the "Societies of Friends and Pro-moters" who have generally taken a particular museum under their care and frequently also organize its events and other activities.

Also among the donors are lottery and tote associations, which convert their own surpluses into cultural donations, and radio and television organizations which waive part of their advertising revenues in favour of museums, and increasingly also industrial and commercial enterprises, which combine sponsorship with more or less unobtrusive image promotion, as well as, in particular, organized civic initiatives which appeal to the public for funds whenever a particular museum event is pending, such as an anniversary, the opening of new rooms or a change of management.

Great patrons of the second half of the 20th century include Josef Haubrich (Cologne), Bernhard Sprengel (Hanover), Karl Ströher (Darmstadt), Wil-helm Hack (Cologne/Ludwigshafen) and Henri Nannen (Emden), who con-verted their private possessions into public property or made them perma-nently accessible to the public. It is no accident that the museums founded on donations generally bear the name of their major donors. Since the early seventies the influence of the sponsoring activities of the Aachen chocolate manufacturer Peter Ludwig has created an especially lasting impression, cooperating with more than a dozen museums, including foreign ones, by making long-term loans available to them which ultimately, so those thus favoured hope, will be converted into foundations. The new building, opened in 1986, of the Wallraf-Richartz-Museum/Museum Ludwig beside Cologne Cathedral is an outstanding result of this kind of cooperation.

Fortunately, during the Second World War the greater part of the endangered collections was stored in safe places in the country, or in mines, and thus protected from extensive capital losses. Museum buildings, on the other hand, were generally either severely damaged or completely destroyed, con-fronting those legally responsible with the task of reconstructing or com-pletely rebuilding them. The fact that this did not start in practice until the 1960s arose from the priorities set for general reconstruction in Germany, which understandably applied in the first place to residential, school, welfare and administrative buildings. After that, opera houses, theatres and concert halls were given preference and only then came the turn of museums and exhibition centres. Thereafter, however, the backlog and the new demands were met at increasing speed, further supported in the old Federal *Länder* by an appeal by the German Research Society (1971) and its "Memorandum on the state of the museums" (1974).

By now it can be recorded that not only have the reparable damages in the museum landscape been largely dealt with, but an impressive number of new buildings and new foundations has already arisen. Since the early sixties the number of museums in the old Federal *Länder* has almost doubled, and even in the new Federal *Länder* it has risen by at least a third. The "Galerie Junge Kunst" (Young Art Gallery) of the Berlin National Gallery was founded in 1965 in Frankfurt/Oder as an independent museum of painting, graphics and sculpture of the then GDR. In 1967 the Brücke Museum, devoted to Central German Expressionism, opened its doors in Berlin. In 1968 came the Modern Gallery of the Saarland Museum in Saarbrücken, in 1970 the East German Gallery in Regensburg, in 1975 the Berlin Gallery and in 1979 both the Wilhelm-Hack-Museum in Ludwigshafen and the Sprengel Museum in Hanover, to name only the major institutions. Reference has already been made to the new foundations of the eighties in Frankfurt am Main.

The museum landscape has blossomed most impressively in North Rhine-Westphalia, the most densely populated *Land* of the Federal Republic of Germany. There, too, the wave of foundations began earlier than elsewhere. In addition to the existing premises came the Schloss Oberhausen Municipal Gallery (1947), the Dortmund Museum am Ostwall (1949), the Gelsenkirchen Municipal Museum and the Recklinghausen Hall of Art, conceived in close association with the Ruhr Festival (both 1950), the Leverkusen Museum Schloss Morsbroich (1951), the Bonn Municipal Museum, with its emphasis on German art since 1945 (1954), the Bochum Museum, focusing on East European moderns (1969), the North Rhine-Westphalia Art Collection in Düsseldorf (1961), the Wilhelm-Lehmbruck-Museum in Duisburg (1964), the Bielefeld Hall of Art (1968), the Aachen Municipal Gallery (1970), the Ludwig Museum in Cologne (1976), which previously existed only as the Modern Department of the Wallraf-Richartz-Museum, the "Quadrat Bottrop" (1976) specializing in constructivist concretist moderns, expanded in 1983 to the Josef-Albers-Museum, and the Ludwig Forum of International Art in Aachen, opened in 1991 in a converted umbrella factory. The planning and execution of the many post-war buildings were debated thoroughly, not only in German and international expert circles, but also by a broad public, especially as the new architecture often produced urban features of an unfamiliar type. This became evident even in Cologne's Wallraf-Richartz-Museum, opened in 1957, the first German museum building after the war (now the Museum of Applied Art) and was soon to continue in the multiform design of the Germanic National Museum in Nuremberg. Similar attention was attracted by the light-flooded Wilhelm-Lehmbruck-Museum in Duisburg, the monumental block of the Bielefeld Hall of Art, the Archiepiscopal Diocesan Museum in Paderborn, which recalls the appearance of a mediaeval shrine, the "historical" solution for the New Pinakothek in Munich and the terrace-like Municipal Museum of Mönchengladbach, slotted into a depression in the slopes of the Abteiberg. Also much talked of were the New State Gallery in Stuttgart, with its dramatic architectural scenery, the Arts and Crafts Museum in Frankfurt am Main, related to the formal language of the Dessau Bauhaus, the strict top lighting system of the North Rhine Westphalian Art Collection, and the overall concept of the Federal Hall of Art and the Municipal Museum in Bonn, developed from the ground plan of a square.

Great attention is also enjoyed by the exhibition premises which do not possess collections of their own but serve as a type of museum providing alternating presentations. These include the communal Halls of Art of Baden-Baden, Berlin, Düsseldorf, Frankfurt am Main, Cologne and Tübingen, the Deichtor Halls for which the Hamburg Cultural Authority is responsible and the new Weserburg Museum, Bremen, opened in 1991, with a programme which is intended to present a repertory of significant private collections of contemporary art. Here too the involvement of business can be successful, as with the Hall of Art of the Hypo Foundation, founded in Munich in 1987 and financed by a bank. There are 334 such exhibition premises in the old Federal *Länder,* most of them in major cities and museum metropolises, where they have become essential features of the living art scene. There are 87 of them in North Rhine-Westphalia, 71 in Baden-Württemberg, 48 in the western section of Berlin, 35 in Lower Saxony and 30 in Bavaria.

The constant increase in museums and exhibition premises has its parallel in a stream of visitors which proves that there can no longer be any question of the notorious "threshold phobia" which once deterred many people from entering the museums, often regarded as a kind of temple. Whereas towards the end of the fifties it was modestly estimated that less than ten million people had visited all the museums of the old Federal *Länder* covered by the statistics, towards the end of the sixties they amounted to some 17 million. By 1975 there were 22 million. Then the figures shot upwards, with 38.5 million visitors in 1979 and 54 million two years later. For 1987 the statistics reported 66 million. Finally, in 1990, after the reunification of Germany, the "magic boundary" of 100 million visitors was passed for the first time in the history of German museums: the museums and exhibition premises in the West of the Federal Republic accounted for more than 79 million and the Eastern Federal *Länder* for up to 24 million. The museums of Natural History, Science and Technology took up the highest proportion of this success with some 19 million, the ethnology and regional museums received over 18 million and the museums of art 17 million visitors, followed at some distance by the historical and archaeological museums with 11 million. However, whereas the demand at folklore and local collections was distributed over nearly 2,000 museums, that is nearly half of the total, in the scientific and technical group it was concentrated on about 600 museums, and as for the art museums, on only a little more than 400 institutes.

Among the most-visited museums in the Federal Republic, with over a million visitors each per year, are currently the German Museum in Munich, the Wallraf-Richartz-Museum/Museum Ludwig in Cologne, the collections of cultural history in Weimar and the Pergamon Museum in Berlin (with the attached buildings containing the Islamic, Near East and Asian art collections).

There are various reasons for the growth in the stream of visitors: in general, the expansion of scholastic and academic educational exhibits, which resulted in an increase in educational demand, the democratization of culture as a whole, and the rise of a leisure society whose interests are partly reflected in cultural tourist activities. Particular causes are the new museum concepts developed since the sixties, with their improved presentation of museum stocks and exhibition objects, as well as the scientifically run didactic and pedagogic aspect of the museums (based chiefly on two recommendations on museum public relations issued by the German UNESCO Commission in 1963). Hand in hand with these are motivations created in the museum environment, as for instance the multiplying art fairs and markets, arts and crafts and other collection fields, which in turn derive from a more intense involvement by the art trade, especially the galleries of classical moderns and contemporary art. Finally, the part played by the mass media cannot be overlooked: the informative reports and critical discussions on radio and television, in daily and weekly papers, journals and illustrated magazines. Art books and volumes of plates with their corresponding themes, published in large editions, together with museum and exhibition catalogues, which have become more and more extensive and rich in content, and have themselves already acquired the status of collectable objects, are playing their part in encouraging and maintaining communication between museums and public.

Among the major supports of a positive balance of visitors are always the special exhibitions. Their numbers have multiplied since the sixties. For 1990, museums throughout the Federal area were able to report 7,100 such events, led by North Rhine-Westphalia with 1,340 special exhibitions. The Bavarian museums followed with 960 and those of Baden-Württemberg with just on 800. Since presentations of this kind not only strengthen the image of the museum concerned but also enhance the prestige of the legal entities involved, that is generally a Federal *Land* or commune, the organizers can always count on special subsidies. Yet it is no secret that in recent years the stretched situation of public budgets has enforced certain restrictions. In many cases, following the example of other Western countries, especially the Americans, there were commercial promoters at hand, industrial firms and trading companies, banks and air lines. Nowadays, public organizers count quite deliberately on such private assistance, for without it many an exhibition would not now take place at all. This applies both to attractive individual presentations and to substantial (often international) travelling exhibitions, for which the insurance payments alone swallow up millions, quite apart from the cost of the years of preparation by qualified organizing teams.

The biggest and most international of all German art exhibitions of the moderns, the "documenta", taking place five-yearly in Kassel, possesses the largest planning staff, linked with permanent archives. First formed in 1955 as a "Museum of the hundred days" and soon promoted to be a seismograph of contemporary art trends (especially of the Western world), it enjoys common financing by the Federation, the *Land* of Hesse and the host city – and naturally also considerable public response. The opening was attended by 130,000 people – a very impressive result in the mid-fifties – but after a continuous rise throughout the eight "documenta", there were already 476,000 in 1987. The fact that such figures are now by no means exceptional is proved from time to time by other events, as for instance the exhibition cycle of "Art circa 1800" initiated by the Hamburg Hall of Art in 1974, which attracted 430,000 visitors, the Darmstadt Jugendstil Retrospective of 1976, with 600,000 visitors, the art exhibition of the Council of Europe, produced under the title "Tendencies of the Twenties" in Berlin in 1977 (345,000 visitors), and the "Hohenstaufen Period" presented in Stuttgart in the same year (800,000 visitors). Also noteworthy are "The Parler and Fine Style 1350–1400 – European Art among the Luxembourgers" in Cologne, 1978 (300,000 visitors) and most recently "Van Gogh and the Moderns", to which some 510,000 visitors poured into Essen in 1990. A record result was achieved by the Tut-ankh-amun Exhibition, shown successively in Cologne, Munich, Hanover and Hamburg in 1980/81: it attracted 1.3 million visitors. Lively attention was and still is aroused by artistic presentations outside the usual exhibition areas, such as the Hanover "Street Art Experiment" of 1970, O.H. Hajek's "Colour Ways" which led in 1985 through the townscape of Bonn, or the "Sculpture Projects in Münster 1987", which were to be seen less as an exhibition than as a work process, because the participating German and foreign artists were realizing their own proposals for the design of selected locations. One of the declared aims of these enterprises is to emphasize the significance of "art in the open space" and to enable wide sections of the population to encounter art in novel ways. The 160 or so art associations, the oldest "Civic Initiatives for Art" carry out an important part of the exhibition work in Germany. It is their traditional task to concern themselves with the latest art of the time, the difficult artists. Generally works are shown by German or foreign artists who are on the threshold of early success or who have already crossed that threshold. The smaller associations comprise up to 800 members, the medium-sized ones up to

2,000 and the large associations up to 4,000 members. With over 7,000 members, the Art Association for the Rhineland and Westphalia in Düsseldorf is not only at the top of the scale; founded in 1829, it is also the oldest of those still in existence. The Art Associations enable their members (who can include both individuals and groups, firms or institutions) to enjoy free entry to all their events, especially the exhibitions, for a minimum annual fee. Moreover, they offer annual gifts, generally consisting of graphics and objects acquired or commissioned from selected artists, and they organize visits to museums, exhibitions or other art-related events (even as far away as America and Asia). Great importance attaches to competition among themselves, but there is also friendly cooperation. For instance, in 1984 the Association of German Art Societies organized a joint show in 46 towns on the theme of "The Art Landscape of the Federal Republic", whose goal was to demonstrate the multiplicity of the contemporary art scene in Germany. In 1991 a project was realized under the title "Art, Europe", in which 63 art societies between Flensburg and Rosenheim took part, with works by young artists from 19 East and West European countries.

However, the artists generally first meet the public through the private art galleries. Whereas there were only a few dozen of these in Germany in the fifties, there are now more than a thousand. There are over a hundred in both Berlin and Cologne. Other focal points are Düsseldorf and Munich. Each gallery organizes its programme according to its individual taste, but is also guided by movements on the international art scene as well as by trends in the market accessible to it. The influential art markets and fairs have become completely essential to the creation and maintenance of contacts. Besides the Cologne "Art Cologne", the first of all the art markets, founded in 1967, there are above all "ART" in Basle, "FIAC" in Paris, "ARCO" in Madrid and "International Art Expo" in Chicago, and the German gallery owners play an important role here. However, in spite of the successes of the German art trade, it should not be overlooked that the majority of galleries, insofar as they have dedicated themselves to the discovery of new artists and the presentation of still unfamiliar work, are working in an insecure margin of the field. The willingness of these enterprises to take risks is remarkable, and a brief life is often the inevitable consequence. But gallery owners are also idealists. Time and again they start afresh and try to gain public acceptance for artists whom the exhibitor values particularly highly. Thus artistic life is constantly regenerated in the private sector as well, and consequently plays a fruitful role in the liveliness and multiplicity of the panorama of exhibitions in the Federal Republic of Germany.

Horst Richter

"Man Walking to the Sky" created by American artist Jonathan Borofsky, became in 1992 the symbol of *documenta IX* in Kassel which attracted 610,000 visitors.

The Museum of Fine Arts established in the former Reich Supreme Court building in Leipzig, which developed out of the Leipzig Art Association, founded in 1837, houses over 2,000 paintings, some 800 sculptures and a graphics collection of more than 55,000 prints.

The Abteiberg Art Museum in Mönchengladbach (North Rhine-Westphalia) is to become a "mecca of the avant-garde". It was built by the Viennese architect Hans Hollein (b. 1934) and handed over to its intended purpose in June, 1982.

Of particular importance is the interplay of private art collectors with the local and regional authorities. As one example of many, the town of Ludwigshafen on the Rhine built a new museum for the private collection of Wilhelm Hack, which is distinguished by significant works of art from the times of the Romans and of the migration of peoples, from the Middle Ages and the 20th century. Our picture shows the ceremonial opening in the presence of the then Federal President Walter Scheel and the Minister-President of Rhineland-Palatinate Bernhard Vogel.

On 4 May, 1984, the German Museum of Architecture was opened on the ▶ Schaumainkai in Frankfurt/Main (Hesse). It was installed in a late 19th century villa converted by Cologne architect Oswald Mathias Ungers. On its left, the Film Museum, another of the buildings housing collections on the so-called "Museum Bank".

The interior courtyard of the New National Gallery in Stuttgart (Baden-Württemberg), opened in 1984. The controversial museum building was designed by the English architect James Stirling.

"Tut-ankh-amun" in the
Cologne City Museum, 1980.

"The Hohenstaufen Period" in
the Württemberg Regional Museum in Stuttgart, 1977.

"Martin Luther and the Re-
formation in the Dukedom of
Prussia" in the National Library
Berlin (West), 1983.

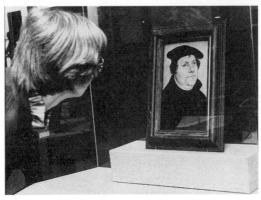

The museums of the Federal Republic of Germany try to attract new groups of visitors
by means of popular special exhibitions. The illustrations on this page must stand for
many others in recalling outstanding exhibition events of the past decade.

The Wallraf-Richartz-Museum/Museum Ludwig, built before the backdrop of the Cologne Cathedral, is one of the many new museum buildings of recent years.

There are numerous museums for specialized collections in every part of the country. In many places there are open-air museums for the preservation of farming culture and techniques, as in the picture above left of the Farmhouse Museum on the Glentleiten above Grossweil in the Bavarian foothills of the Alps. On the subject of technology, the German Museum in Munich (top right) has one of the largest collections in the world.

The Painting Gallery of Old Masters in Dresden is among the most important art collections in Europe. The building, sited directly on the Zwinger, was constructed by Gottfried Semper from 1847 to 1854.

Goethe's garden house in Weimar's Ilmpark is open to the public as a literary memorial. Below: a view of Goethe's study. Goethe worked on *Wilhelm Meister, Iphigenie* and *Tasso* at the high desk in the background.

The "feudal heritage" of theatre in the Federal Republic of Germany: a view of the auditorium of the old Residence Theatre in Munich, also known as the "Cuvilliés Theatre" after its builder François de Cuvilliés (1695–1768) (above). Below left, the Munich National Theatre, first built in 1811 and re-opened after war damage in 1963, home of the Bavarian State Opera. Below right: built on the pattern of the Bayreuth Festival Theatre, the Prinzregententheater, also in Munich, which has just been partially restored and used for productions again since the beginning of 1988.

Theatre

In the Federal Republic of Germany cultural multiplicity is especially evident in the theatre, the structure, variety and financial security of which defy comparison.

The tradition of feudally-influenced court theatres, the theatres of cities and principal towns, goes far back into the 18th century. When the First World War put an end to the German Empire and its princedoms, the public authorities took charge of the theatres, and towns and states took on their management apparently as a matter of course. And thus, in the time of the Weimar Republic, the currently so broadly diversified system of German theatres developed, which is, on the one hand, subsidized by the *Länder* and local authorities and, on the other, guarantees a high degree of independence and sole responsibility to its managers. Despite their great financial dependence, they can always appeal to the freedom of the arts as enshrined in the Constitution of the Federal Republic of Germany.

In the late 80s, the 85 municipal and state theatres run by the local authorities and the *Länder* of the former Federal Republic and currently performing on some 200 stages were supported to the tune of a total of 1.7 thousand million DM. Without these subsidies, which allow a high artistic standard and cover 85% of the huge and still-rising personnel expenditure, none of them could exist, for no more than an average of 17% of the expenditure is returned via the entrance fees paid at the box office (with an average of 72% take-up of seats at the drama theatre and 83% at the musical theatre).

Similar conditions prevail with the theatres of the former GDR, which in different political circumstances (and for different reasons) enjoyed equally generous support. When one compares the number of theatre seats with the population figures, the East German part-state appears as the richest theatre country in the world: 60 theatres, including 30 opera companies, offered their performances at more than 120 locations. Considerable state subventions made sure that the admission prices charged were astonishingly low. Today scarcely anyone can believe that the most expensive ticket giving admission to the magnificent building of the East Berlin State Opera Unter den Linden cost only 15 GDR marks. The state administration and ideological control of cultural life in general, however, tolerated neither private theatres on a commercial basis nor those Free Groups whose willingness to experiment stimulated the established theatre elsewhere.

In the old Federal *Länder,* on the other hand, touring theatre and travelling guest companies in nearly 300 towns ensured an almost nationwide, regular supply of professional performing art. Apart from the flourishing festivals organized only on a seasonal basis, and countless amateur theatres, theatres in the old Federal Republic welcome annual audiences of some 27 million; of these 4 million fall to the touring companies and an equal amount to the stationary private theatres principally devoted to entertainment and existing only on small subsidies, or none; the so-called Free Groups, largely mobile and independent in their programmes as well as financially, which direct their attention to experimental or political forms of theatre, receive about a million visitors.

Since the Second World War and the phase of reconstruction of more than a hundred theatres destroyed by the war, it has not only been the big cities of Berlin (West) and Munich, Hamburg and Cologne which, with the definite advantage of the federative system of the Federal Republic of Germany, have been competing for leadership in the theatrical arts. From time to time, theatre cities such as Frankfurt and Stuttgart, Ulm and Bochum, Kassel and Bremen have also worked their way well to the fore. In the GDR, on the other hand, Berlin continued its uncontested domination as the arbiter of quality and trend-setting theatrical metropolis to which a continuous stream of talented recruits poured from the theatres of the country. Nevertheless, in the course of the years regional theatrical centres, such as Halle, Potsdam, Schwerin, Karl-Marx-Stadt (Chemnitz) and Dresden offered successful competition to the capital.

The prestigious, but also the aesthetic significance of the Bayreuth Festival is unbroken. It is dedicated exclusively to the work of its creator, the musical dramas of Richard Wagner. Under the management of Wieland (d. 1966) and Wolfgang Wagner, the composer's two grandsons, its style has twice undergone profound changes: first in the 50s, influenced especially by the director Wieland Wagner, whose symbolism did away with the old naturalistic and emotional forms of presentation and, as the "New Bayreuth Style", made operatic history. Since the 70s, the most important productions at Bayreuth have become realistic again. Particular excitement was aroused by the productions of the tetralogy *The Ring of the Nibelung* in 1976 under the direction of Patrice Chéreau from France (with Pierre Boulez as conductor) and in 1988 under the GDR director Harry Kupfer (with Daniel Barenboim conducting).

If Bayreuth represents the classical type of the middle- and upper-class festival, which has nevertheless brought its programme up to date, then attempts were being made in Recklinghausen in the Ruhr area to establish new traditions after the Second World War. From the solidarity of the miners with the impoverished theatre shortly after the war, the Ruhr Festival developed, supported by the German Trade Unions Federation and the town of Recklinghausen, paying off the actors' old debt of gratitude with the slogan "Art for Coal" and with the aim of stressing the social obligations of the arts. With the democratic principle in mind that art is cultural education and is there for everyone, highly qualified guest performances and productions, and from the early 80s also performances by a small company based in the Ruhr district, were offered predominantly via employee-run enterprises. Even more popular than the frequently criticized and crisis-ridden Ruhr Festival are the summertime open-air theatres playing against natural and urban backdrops, in beautiful squares, forts, stairways, in forests and ruins. They attract visitors – in the West to Bad Gandersheim and Bad Hersfeld, to Wunsiedel, Jagsthausen and Schwäbisch Hall, and in the East to the Bergtheater Thale in the Harz and to the Rathen Felsenbühne – audiences which include many holidaymakers and tourists, who scarcely ever visit the theatre during the rest of the year.

If we take a look at the programmes of the four decades of theatre since the beginning of the division of Germany, certain phases are particularly striking. After the chaos left behind by the National Socialist regime and the Second World War, the desire for theatre was surprisingly great, in the hope of diversion, but also of a healing of the spirit. Theatres and mini-theatres shot up like mushrooms; at times there were performances on two hundred improvised stages in Berlin alone. With the beginning of the Cold War and the increasingly rigorous division of Germany, the theatre in the two states moved along more and more distinctly separate paths. In the theatre season of 1948/49, the first after the Currency Reform, when conditions began to stabilize, one particular drama was staged in the West, which was concerned with resistance and sabotage in the Third Reich: Carl Zuckmayer's *The Devil's General* – 53 theatres gave it a total of more than two thousand performances in that season.

In the same period, however, 22 theatres put on Goethe's *Faust,* and there were actually 78 different productions of Shakespeare's plays. Wolfgang Borchert's late-expressionist homecoming drama *The Man Outside* had a marked influence, while one classical post-war drama, Lessing's *Minna von Barnhelm,* has remained the front-runner of all plays to this day.

The leaders in the field of operetta are Johann Strauss with *Fledermaus* and *Gipsy Baron,* Franz Lehár with *The Merry Widow* and *Land of Smiles,* and Emmerich Kálmán with *Countess Mariza* and *Csárdás Princess.* But increasingly, the musical is replacing interest in the old favourites, the operetta giving way to *My Fair Lady* and *Fireworks, Kiss me Kate, Fiddler on the Roof,* and *Cats.*

In the opera, on the other hand, as far as choice of works is concerned, there were few changes. The repertoire is maintained, and to an overwhelming extent it derives from the late 18th and the 19th century.

Mozart, Wagner and Verdi, Lortzing and Puccini ranked ahead of Richard Strauss and far ahead of the "classical" new music of Alban Berg, ahead of Paul Hindemith, Hans Werner Henze and Gottfried von Einem, ahead of Bernd Alois Zimmermann, Udo Zimmermann and Wolfgang Rihm. Despite many premières and many a composition commissioned by the great opera houses (for instance Aribert Reimann's *Lear,* Munich, 1978), contemporary musical theatre has very seldom found lasting admission to the programmes. Movement came to the opera houses especially through well-known theatre directors, Hans Hollmann and Rudolf Noelte, Adolf Dresen and Hansgünther Heyme, Jürgen Flimm, Luc Bondy, Alfred Kirchner and Jürgen Gosch, Peter Stein and Klaus Michael Grüber, and, perhaps the best example of all, through Hans Neuenfels and his *Aida* in Frankfurt (1981). All of them brought theatrical imagination and often also experimental bravura to works long regarded as no more than museum treasures. Successes begin to emerge: interest in the genre is growing, even among younger people.

After the years of dealing with the past in theatre, the more poetic and philosophical plays from France and England became much sought after. Jean-Paul Sartre, Albert Camus, Jean Anouilh and Jean Giraudoux, George Bernard Shaw, T. S. Eliot and Christopher Fry were the authors, until Max Frisch and Friedrich Dürrenmatt made their mark among the German-speaking authors along with Carl Zuckmayer. In the 50s the boom of the so-called Theatre of the Absurd began, with the arrival of plays by Eugène Ionesco and above all by Samuel Beckett, which held the stage for a long time as witnesses to helplessness and resignation.

Most of the authors referred to remained unknown to theatre enthusiasts in East Germany for decades; nevertheless a dramatic art developed there which also exerted an influence on the West and in many respects left traces on world theatre. Trusting in the anti-Fascist democratic new beginning proclaimed by the Soviet occupying power and the ruling German Communists, many artists took up residence, after their emigration, in the Soviet zone of occupation, which in 1949 became the "GDR". From Switzerland, where in the Nazi period they had belonged to the legendary Zurich Playhouse ensemble, came Wolfgang Langhoff, Wolfgang Heinz and (for a time) Karl Paryla. Together and successively they constituted three decades of artistic development in the Berlin German Theatre, following on the traditions created by former directors Otto Brahm, Max Reinhardt and Heinz Hilpert. From the USA (via Switzerland) came Bertolt Brecht, who founded the Berliner Ensemble in 1949.

Dissatisfied with a dramatic art which (according to him) was dominated by externals and a false sincerity, he called for a new theatre which would help to shape the world itself. "Intervention theatre" in Brecht's sense was introduced in the first première of the Berliner Ensemble, with Brecht's play

Mother Courage and her Children. Artistically, the completely new epic mode of performance that Brecht had developed shocked and fascinated: the half-raised curtain, the inclusion of songs, the "narrative arrangement", the apparently cool, dry art of dialogue presentation. But at the same time the public also had to face a thoroughly uncomfortable message: in the ruined city of Berlin, Brecht taunted the Germans, who after the war was lost consoled themselves that they had been fighting for lofty national ideals: in war it's only business that matters and "the little man has no profit".

The official cultural policy of the GDR was at first by no means prepared to concede the rank of a "theatre of the new age" (as the writer himself evaluated it) to Brecht's theatre, which was regarded as brittle, grey and decadently bourgeois. All his life Brecht had to defend himself in the GDR against violent attacks from those responsible for cultural policy. His plays were scarcely performed except by the Berliner Ensemble, and it was not until the triumphant foreign guest performances by the Ensemble, especially at the festival "Theatre of the Nations" in Paris, that the Berliner Ensemble achieved recognition and increasing appreciation from the public in the GDR as well.

When he died in 1956, Brecht's pupils Benno Besson, Manfred Wekwerth and Peter Palitzsch developed his methods, so that despite all the sceptical forecasts the Berliner Ensemble not only continued to exist without its founder and spiritual mentor, but from the mid-fifties to the mid-sixties reached the peak of its international influence. Performances such as *The Irresistible Rise of Arturo Ui* (1959), *The Days of the Commune* (1962) and *Coriolanus* (1963) left their demonstrable effects everywhere. Brecht's pupils of the second and third generation, such as Manfred Karge, Matthias Langhoff and B.K. Tragelehn, exerted a marked influence on the further development of theatre in the GDR and also enriched the dramatic art of the old Federal Republic, after they had moved there to avoid the repression in the East. The great father figure corresponding to Brecht in the development of the musical theatre in the GDR was Walter Felsenstein. At the Comic Opera in East Berlin founded by him in 1947 he declared war on the "costumed concert" of singing stars posing on the stage. Following up the efforts at reform of the twenties, he used song and acting as media of equal merit for the same dramatic events and in this way achieved a "re-theatricalization" of the opera. Ridiculed initially as a dreamer trying to transfer to the operatic stage criteria which were alien to the genre, Felsenstein ultimately convinced his opponents. In the Comic Opera "workshop" scholarly backing and thorough, unusually long rehearsals led to performances of impressive theatrical merit, such as: *The Cunning Little Fox, The Magic Flute, Othello* and *Tales of Hoffmann.* Felsenstein was followed by such directors as Joachim Herz, Götz Friedrich and Harry Kupfer, who later enriched the German and international musical theatre with their own musical theatre projects. Kupfer in particular developed at the Comic Opera in the eighties a particularly lively, imaginative form of the modern musical theatre with its contemporary criticism (*The Mastersingers of Nuremberg, Boris Godunov, Lear, Giustino, Orpheus and Eurydice,* the Mozart cycle). Ruth Berghaus, on the other hand, took her inspiration from Brecht's aesthetics and her teacher, the famous dancer Gret Palucca, and enriched the operatic scene with a productive alternative blueprint. Her productions at the German State Opera Berlin (including the premières of the Dessau operas *Puntila, Lancelot, Einstein*) became style-setters.

In the old Federal Republic the theatre was associated with prestige, an attitude which predominated until the early sixties, guided mainly by directors of the type and aura of a Gustaf Gründgens. The incipient change was indicated in 1963 by Rolf Hochhuth's *The Representative,* the complaint against the Pope's role during the period of Jewish persecution by National Socialism. This was followed by a number of other documentary plays: Heinar Kipphardt's *In the Matter of J. Robert Oppenheimer,* Tankred Dorst's *Toller,* the *Discourse on Vietnam,* and *The Investigation* by Peter Weiss. Still stimulated by Erwin Piscator, the politically-oriented man of the theatre, they were already associated with the politicization of the theatre, which became apparent in the late sixties under the influence of the campaigns of revolutionary students.

A decade of retreat followed, with a new sensitivity on the stage. As early as 1973, a play by the Austrian Peter Handke, who wrote his famous *Attack on the Public* in 1966, was performed. The play, which recommended understanding even for the feelings of the capitalists, is entitled *They are Dying Out.* Programmatics and agitprop, which had led to a major loss of audiences, generally gave way once again to the presentation of the scruples, contradictions, and incalculability of the human being, including, of course, doubts about the power of dramatic art to change anything.

At the same time, new, younger German-speaking authors appeared, critical realists such as Wolfgang Bauer, Harald Sommer and Peter Turrini, who primarily emphasized the artificiality of our lives and our artistic usages. Referring back to the long-forgotten dramatic works of Brecht's pupil Marieluise Fleisser, came Rainer Werner Fassbinder, Martin Sperr, and above all Franx Xaver Kroetz, authors who arraigned the coldness in human and social relationships and took up the cause of the unknown and the underprivileged. In contrast, Dieter Forte's *Martin Luther & Thomas Münzer,* misrepresenting history, offered a radical, theatrical reckoning with early capitalism.

Among the women authors, the Austrian Elfriede Jelinek became the partisan of the weaker sex with her emancipatory plays, while Gerlind Reinshagen and Friederike Roth used decidedly more tender and sometimes lyrical forms of theatre for subjects of social criticism. Besides Kroetz, an exceptional phenomenon of contemporary theatre is Botho Strauss. No other playwright expresses the change of mood from political and socio-critical commitment to the individual psychological image of time and character with as much significance as he does. Strauss, born in 1944, was still playing his part as a forceful drama critic in the 60s; then, as dramatic adviser to director Peter Stein, he influenced and sensitively developed the Berlin Schaubühne, the leading theatre of the 70s; as playwright, however, he has since been a seismographic recorder of the perils, the identity crisis of modern man due to depersonalized, functional behaviour patterns.

Much-performed and typical of the divergent stylistic trends of the 80s were Heiner Müller and the recently deceased Thomas Bernhard, the two leading contemporary dramatists of the GDR and Austria respectively; Müller, following Brecht, with a constant output of cryptic texts on German history and the German-German present, Bernhard in the baroque tradition with tragicomedies on the transitory nature and frailty of man. It is only in the most recent past that some authors have reacted critically to the founding years of the Federal Republic (Klaus Pohl, Harald Kuhlmann, Michael Schneider), while Harald Mueller's *Totenfloss,* the play of the year in 1986, presented a vision of the world after the nuclear catastrophe, corresponding to the current apocalyptic attitudes. Finally, the first dramatic reflexes of German reunification are to be found in Klaus Pohl's *Karate-Billi Comes Back* and Botho Strauss's much-performed *Final Chorus* (1990).

At least as important to theatrical life in the Federal Republic, sometimes superseding attention to younger authors, are, however, the mighty, prominent directors. In fact, the aesthetically most appealing productions have frequently arisen from risky, often extremely unconventional approximations (by Peter Zadek, Ernst Wendt, Claus Peymann, and many more) to the classics. The catchword for this is director's theatre: an advance over the literalization of the older theatre and a problem owing to the tendency to forced originality.

Director's theatre was and is closely bound up with artistic innovations in the field of stage decor. While interest in the performing human being, in the actor's personality, has been growing again in very recent times, the Federal German theatre has revived since the late 60s, above all thanks to important stage designers, some now themselves directing (Wilfried Minks, Thomas Richter-Forgách, Karl-Ernst Herrmann, Rolf Glittenberg, Erich Wonder, Achim Freyer) and has been revolutionized as regards visual material.

In the former GDR the repertoire was determined largely by the official cultural policy. The required 'balanced programme' consisted as a rule of one-third of works by the classical writers, from antiquity via Shakespeare, Goldoni and Molière to Goethe, Schiller and Kleist, a further third devoted to the so-called critical realists (Ibsen, Chekhov, Gerhart Hauptmann, Wedekind and Kaiser) and one third reserved for contemporary drama. One première per season of a play created in the GDR, or the first performance of a new foreign language play was regarded as the duty of every theatre.

State control of the programme policy ensured on the one hand a varied and literarily demanding supply of plays. On the other hand, censorship suppressed whole areas of world literature. Certain tendencies of West European drama had long been regarded as bourgeois decadent and ideologically hostile. Above all, it was a long time before the dramatists of the Absurd: Beckett, Ionesco and even Giraudoux, Anouilh and Genet, the modern American and East European authors influenced by the Western Moderns, were allowed to be performed on the stages of the former GDR. The result was that the theatre enthusiasts in the GDR did not see a key drama such as Beckett's *Waiting for Godot* until 25 years after its première. But censorship was particularly obstinate in relation to GDR authors who critically opposed the socialism that actually existed. The chief works of Heiner Müller, Volker Braun and Christoph Hein did not appear on GDR stages until many years after they were written, in some cases more than a decade later. The more the state came to oppose the ideals that it theoretically proclaimed, the more the GDR theatre grew into the role of an unofficial opposition. Anything that was not allowed to be expressed in the newspapers and the electronic media was handled in more or less encoded form in the theatre. A coded language was developed, making use of the works of classical writers in particular. For instance, Goethe's *Torquato Tasso,* in which he deals with the contradiction between mind and might, was used to oppose the illegal expulsion of song-writer Wolf Biermann. A performance of *Wilhelm Tell* had the effect of an open call to resistance in the last year of the GDR: "The old is passing, the times are changing now!" GDR theatres assumed the function of the "conscience of the nation", which meant that a major role was assigned to them in the popular opposition movement in 1989.

Two plays whose premières finally took place after long struggles against Party opposition introduced the end of the GDR: in Volker Braun's *Übergangsgesellschaft* the old Communist Wilhelm gives this résumé of existence: "Revolution cannot succeed as a dictatorship. If we do not liberate ourselves there is nothing there for us. There is no compensation for past injustice." At the courageous first performance in the Berlin Maxim Gorky Theatre (director: Thomas Langhoff) the audience held their breath at these phrases. At the same time, the Dresden State Theatre, in the play *Die Ritter der Tafelrunde* by Christoph Hein (director: Klaus-Dieter Kirst) showed the members of the aging Politbüro of the SED as a load of peevish old men, long isolated from the outside world, concerned only with maintaining their own power. Only one continues to seek the Grail (the Communist ideal?) and does not find it ... The same theatre, which Brecht had exhorted 40 years earlier to change the world, had now actually made its contribution to changing the world.

At the beginning of the nineties theatres were seeking their new function and identity in the area of the new Federal *Länder*. An unimpeded exchange between West German and East German theatre folk promises mutual enrichment, and we can expect interesting future developments. We shall be able as before to study their results in two "shop windows" every year: for the authors' theatre at the Mülheim Theatre Days, which have been putting on new German plays since 1976, and for directors' theatre at the Berlin Theatre Meeting, which has now been selecting the most remarkable productions (in the view of a board of critics) for a quarter of a century.

Dietmar N. Schmidt/Dieter Kranz

"Mother Courage brings the shoes in which it's easier to run": Helene Weigel sings the "Courage Song" at the première for the founding of the Berliner Ensemble 1949 with Bertolt Brecht's play *Mother Courage and her Children* (with Angelika Hurwicz as Dumb Kattrin, Ekkehard Schall as Eilif and Heinz Schubert as Swiss Cheese).

For political reasons, Heiner Müller (b. 1929), the most important dramatist of the ▶ GDR since Brecht, was performed almost exclusively in the Federal Republic until the mid-eighties. The illustration shows a scene from *Germania Tod in Berlin,* here the première production by the Munich Kammerspiele in 1978 (directed by Ernst Wendt): a play which dramatizes German history from the end of the First World War until the early years of the GDR using tragicomic, grotesque means.

Heiner Müller's *The Battle,* produced by Manfred Karge and Matthias Langhoff at the East Berlin People's Theatre: the performance takes place on the apron, surrounded by the audience, sitting both in the auditorium and in the stage house itself.

In 1985, Klaus Michael Grüber, perhaps the most subjective of German theatre directors, produced Shakespeare's tragedy *King Lear* at the Schaubühne Berlin with Bernhard Minetti in the title-role; on the left, Branko Samarovski as Edgar, on the right, Peter Roggisch as Gloucester.

Sophocles' *Oedipus* under the direction of Jürgen Gosch at the Hamburg Thalia-Theater: an attempt to save the forms of Greek tragedy and to carry them over into the present in a theatrically moving way, to revive them with masks, dance, and buskin.

Shakespeare's *Macbeth* as dance drama, choreographically narrated by Hans Kresnik at the Städtische Bühnen in Heidelberg. The première in the spring of 1988 made clear reference to the unscrupulous rise and fall of the politician Uwe Barschel.

Dramatist Heiner Müller's treatment and production of *Macbeth* at the East Berlin People's Theatre in 1982: the story of the struggle for power became the artistic image of a world governed by force and brutality. The part of Macbeth was divided among three actors: Dieter Montag (right), Michael Gwisdek (left) and Hermann Beyer.

Critical theatre from the Württemberg National Theatre in Stuttgart, where in 1967 Peter Palitzsch, a pupil of Brecht, produced Shakespeare's trilogy *King Henry VI* on two evenings as a grandiose, frivolous, deadly game of the powerful, entitled *The War of the Roses*.

Since 1951, the thousand-year old Romanesque convent ruins of Bad Hersfeld have housed festivals under the patronage of the President of the Federal Republic: especially open-air performances of classical plays, a summer theatre of changing artistic success and ambition, but always of the greatest interest to the audience.

The Ruhr Festival, financed by the German Trade Unions Federation (DGB) and the town of Recklinghausen in North Rhine-Westphalia, is the central focus and the highlight of union cultural activity. For eight weeks in every year, the Ruhr Festival Theatre in Recklingshausen becomes the place where artists and workers meet. Shown here: a scene from *Lysistrata* in a production by Heinz Engels.

Botho Strauss (b. 1944) is one of the authors who have managed to define and, with linguistic creativity, to formulate – on the stage – the feelings of the age and the intellectual horizon of society in the Federal Republic of Germany. Following Shakespeare's *Midsummer Night's Dream,* he wrote the *Park,* a journey through the erotic mythology of the present. Shown here are two scenes from Dieter Dorn's production at the Munich Kammerspiele, with Edgar Selge and Jutta Hoffmann above and Romuald Pekny and Manfred Zapatka below.

One of the most discussed directors in the Federal Republic since the mid-sixties has been Peter Zadek, historically important particularly for his Shakespeare productions: the illustration shows *Othello*. 1976, at the Deutsches Schauspielhaus in Hamburg, with Ulrich Wildgruber in the title-role and Eva Mattes as Desdemona.

Mein Kampf by George Tabori had its German première in the 87/88 season at the Städtische Bühnen in Dortmund under the direction of Guido Huonder: scenes from a Viennese men's refuge, in which the Jew Herzl, God, Death, and Hitler tell their strange, ridiculous, and terrible stories.

Gaston Salvatore, a relation of the murdered Chilean President Allende working in the Federal Republic of Germany, wrote the two-character play *Stalin,* in which the Soviet dictator, during the last days of his life, holds conversations with a prominent, intimidated actor and portrayer of Lear. Photograph from Heribert Sasse's première production at the Berlin Schillertheater in the 87/88 season with Rolf Henniger (left) and Eberhard Müller-Elmau as Stalin.

The *Nibelungenlied,* often described as the German national epic and myth, was dramatized in the mid-19th century by Friedrich Hebbel and has recently returned to the stage: the illustration shows a scene from the excellent performance of the *Nibelungen* at the Thalia Theatre in Hamburg (1988, Director Jürgen Flimm) with Hans Kremer as Siegfried and Hildegard Schmal as Brunhild.

The play of the theatre season 1986/87: *Totenfloss* by Harald Mueller, a dramatic reaction to the nuclear catastrophe at Chernobyl, which was performed on more than two dozen stages within a very brief period. In the photograph: Ellen Schulz and Matthias Leja in Dietrich Hilsdorf's Frankfurt production.

Anton Chekhov's *Three Sisters* was produced by Peter Stein at the Berlin Schaubühne in 1984: a model production in the sense of a performance faithful to text and milieu, and balanced in atmosphere. The actresses were Jutta Lampe (Masha), Corinna Kirchhoff (Irina), Edith Clever (Olga).

In 1985, Volker Ludwig's musical *Linie I* was given its première at the Berlin Grips-Theater, which plays an exemplary role among German theatres for children and young people with its critically entertaining realism: scenes from a revue between the stations of an underground line.

A naked foot symbolizing cobbler Hans Sachs dominates Carl-Friedrich Oberle's stage-set for the "Festive Meadow" in Act 3 of Richard Wagner's *Meistersinger* in Jaroslav Chundela's Essen production in 1988. Heinz Wallberg was musical director.

The rediscovery and rehabilitation of Jacques Offenbach's "Opera bouffe" *Sir Bluebeard* was one of the great achievements of director Walter Felsenstein at the Comic Opera in East Berlin. In the 1963 production Hanns Nocker sang Bluebeard, Anny Schlemm Boulotte and Werner Enders King Bobeche.

Ruth Berghaus is the internationally best-known female opera director of the former GDR. The illustration shows Peter Schreier as Almaviva and Rainer Süss as Dr. Bartolo in her production of Rossini's *The Barber of Seville* at the Berlin Stage Opera Unter den Linden in 1968.

The final scene of Modest Mussorgsky's *Boris Godunov* at the Comic Opera in East Berlin, produced by Felsenstein's successor Harry Kupfer. Siegfried Vogel sang Boris and alto singer Jochen Kowalski began his international career as his son Feodor.

Viehjud Levi is a part of the process of overcoming the past in the everyday environment of a village. The play by Thomas Strittmatter was produced by Kai Braak in Freiburg in the 86/87 season and subsequently also presented at the Berlin Theatre Meeting – a critics' selection of the best productions.

"Tanzabend II" in the 85/86 season in Wuppertal: one of the two annual new productions with which choreographer Pina Bausch has created a new world of dance theatre in the years since 1973.

"The revolution cannot succeed as a dictatorship. There is no compensation for past injustice" – the verdict on the GDR, spoken by a disappointed old-time communist in Volker Braun's *Übergangsgesellschaft,* which was performed at the East Berlin Maxim-Gorky Theatre in a production by Thomas Langhoff.

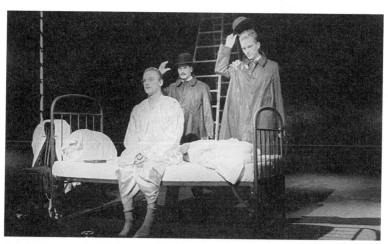

Der neue Prozess by Peter Weiss (1916–82), dramatized on the basis of Franz Kafka's novel *The Trial,* was performed in the 1986/87 season under the direction of Roberto Ciulli in the Theater an der Ruhr, which has its seat in Mülheim, from where, with its ambitious productions, it constitutes a serious rival to the commercial touring theatre-companies.

As early as 1959, the famous Finnish architect Alvar Aalto (1898–1976) designed an opera house for the city of Essen in the Ruhr-district. Whereas elsewhere in the Federal Republic a theatre building-boom broke out in the sixties and seventies, the plans for Essen lay dormant for lack of funds and were realized only posthumously in the eighties. The illustrations show an exterior view and a view of the foyers of the opera house, which opened on 25 September, 1988.

Theatre buildings between functionality and prestige: above, the Düsseldorf Schauspielhaus, built by B. Pfau in 1960–69; below, the reconstructed Semper Opera House in Dresden, which was destroyed in the war and rebuilt according to Gottfried Semper's original plans.

Johann Sebastian Bach as scarcely anyone has seen him: this refreshingly disrespectful portrait of the man who was to be choirmaster of St. Thomas's was made by sculptor Bernd Göbel (b. 1942) for Arnstadt in Thuringia, where the young Bach was employed as an organist from 1703 to 1707 and according to local tradition was involved in quite a number of affrays.

Music

With the deaths of Richard Strauss (born 1864) and Hans Pfitzner (born 1869), the year 1949 – the year when the two separate states of Germany were established after the Second World War – marks the end of a late and post-romantic musical tradition that had continued to govern the musical life of the "Third Reich", which attempted to restore the "old order". The manufacture of an approach, which would be justified on the grounds of composition, to a de-romanticized musical future was the task with which the composers of the Federal Republic of Germany and the GDR were both faced. And yet developments in the two countries were very divergent at first, although in the last years before reunification they gradually began to converge again. In the West, Darmstadt (Hesse), with the "International Holiday Courses for New Music" which had taken place there annually since 1946, became the centre for debate. In the immediate post-war years interest focused on following up the vehement, anti-emotional German music of the twenties, the neo-baroque objective style of Paul Hindemith (1895–1963) and the great key figure of Igor Stravinsky. Yet the young composers – such as Bernd Alois Zimmermann (1918–1970), Giselher Klebe (born 1925), pupil of Josef Rufer, and Hans Werner Henze (born 1926), who achieved rapid distinction – soon realized as they exchanged views with guests of similar age from Italy (Bruno Maderna, Luigi Nono, and later Luciano Berio), France (Pierre Boulez), and England (Peter Racine Fricker), that the changed historical situation demanded a new approach.

Even for the older people, who were teaching in Darmstadt or were performed there, and who were still to some extent influenced by the Hindemith style, a phase of unreserved rethinking of their positions now began: for instance in the case of Wolfgang Fortner (1907–1987) or Boris Blacher (1903–1975) or Karl Amadeus Hartmann (1905–1963), reactivated after total "inner emigration". In the search for tenable, logically conclusive methods of composition, which, more than from Schönberg's twelve-tone method itself, received its inspiration from Anton Webern's structural conclusions resulting therefrom, Karlheinz Stockhausen (born 1928) soon emerged as an inventive stimulator. And since he was flexible and open enough to accept the demands of the time and translate them, as a composer, into a tonal language of his own – whether in terms of the newly-discovered electronic sounds, the anarchic tendencies of the American John Cage, or of the opening up of space, of improvisation, and open form, or the idea of "world music" – Stockhausen (alongside Henze, who was quite differently situated and took up permanent residence in Italy in 1953) became one of the internationally best-known composers and representatives of German contemporary music, who wants to create a visionary music drama of Wagnerian dimensions with his monumental weekday cycle *Licht,* which is intended to be finished by the year 2003. Vital aesthetic impulses continued to emerge from the so-called Darmstadt School right up to the end of the sixties – until the death of the music sociologist, philosopher, and composer Theodor W. Adorno; regarding such impulses, we must of course include those composers who, despite their kinship as regards compositional means and aesthetic ambitions, were more distinguished for their critical distance from every kind of group-forming. These include Mauricio Kagel (born in Buenos Aires in 1931), working in the Federal Republic of Germany, or György Ligeti (born in 1923 in the part of Hungary that now belongs to Romania) or even those outsiders who assumed a characteristic anti-attitude directed against the newly-established music business or even against the ivory tower of the musical avant-garde: Helmut Lachenmann (born 1935), Hans Joachim Hespos (born 1938), Wilhelm Killmayer (born 1927), Nicolaus A. Huber (born 1939), Josef Anton Riedl (born 1927), or Dieter Schnebel (born 1930). The latest generation of composers born after the war, who are again taking up tonal and traditional elements as well as love of extended forms and big orchestras, seems to have established itself relatively quickly as a group; Wolfgang Rihm, Peter Michael Hamel, Hans-Jürgen von Bose, Detlev Müller-Siemens (this should probably include Volker David Kirchner, born in 1942). Superficially, the group appears united by a curious lack of historical awareness in the adoption of various, even obsolete musical materials and forms. However, when one looks at the style of their works, some of these composers are today divided by as much as Schönberg and Stravinsky, those great opposites from the pioneer days of musical modernism, once were.

Peter Michael Hamel's works, for instance, in which preoccupation with the minimalist principles of composition of a Steve Reich, but also the improvisation practised by jazz and rock music, as well as the meditative mood of an "Asiatically" inspired mental attitude (also initiated by Jean Gebser) have left their mark, may perhaps be compared with the Zen-Buddhist-oriented projects of Walter Zimmermann, aiming at mixing cultures, but scarcely with the opulent, quasi-romantic orchestral works of a Wolfgang Rihm, created with the utmost tonal refinement.

If we now look briefly at the musical history of the GDR, the characteristic differences can be attributed to basic patterns similar to those in the other areas of cultural activity. Developments took place in the fifties and sixties, the period of the Cold War, largely in isolation, cut off from international exchange. New methods of composition such as the aleatoric approach, inspired by Pierre Boulez with his famous "Alea Lecture" in Darmstadt in 1957, did not reach the GDR until the late sixties, making a paradoxical detour via Poland where a free spirit reigned in musical matters and composers such as Witold Lutosławski and Krzysztof Penderecki had arrived at similar methods. Meanwhile in the GDR, even in music the dogma of "socialist realism" prevailed, favouring an easily comprehensible, ideologically charged political utility music. The historical point of linkage after the Second World War was the work of the two great socialist composers Hanns Eisler (1898–1962) and Paul Dessau (1894–1979), who returned from their exile in America and put their work entirely at the service of the new state (though even they were not spared the accusation of "formalism" and disciplinary action by the Party).

Although a certain amount of liberalization occurred in the seventies and eighties, it must be regarded as a special achievement under such working conditions that a considerable number of composers of the former GDR kept in touch with international developments and were able to make independent contributions. A few names must represent them all: Ruth Zechlin (born 1926), Reiner Bredemeyer (1929), Siegfried Matthus (1934), Georg Katzer (1935), Rainer Kunad (1936), Tilo Medek (1940), Friedrich Schenker (1942) and Udo Zimmermann (1943), whose opera *Die weisse Rose,* about the Scholls, executed in the "Third Reich" as resistance fighters, is among the most-performed works of the German musical theatre of recent years.

Jazz, as the most American of all musical trends, became a special indicator of political division in the Germany of the post-war decades. Regarded in the East with suspicion and tolerated only as a reluctant concession to youth, it became for its supporters a kind of secret declaration of independence. In the West, on the other hand, it assumed a pace-making role in the fifties for that general Americanization of popular culture which has governed successive decades until now. In jazz especially, the page was really turned. The dependence of German jazz musicians on the once all-powerful and style-setting American models was overcome in recent years, following the new confidence felt by Europeans in themselves, but also owing to better economic conditions for jazz musicians in Europe. But there are other, more inherently musical reasons for the emancipation of European jazz musicians from their American mentors. With the rise of Free Jazz in the early sixties, for the first time the musical ideal was not a style but rather a non-conformist artistic attitude of mind; no precise tonal structures or compositional norms, but a conglomerate of individual styles expressing a latent "contra" rather than an open "pro". Music which proclaims non-conformism as its goal simultaneously does away with ideals: for the Free Jazz musicians of

Europe, there was nothing left to copy, not even the old hierarchy of accompanists and soloists, stars and ensembles, improvisers and background musicians. Collective improvisation became important. Particularly significant for German Free Jazz was the influence of the circle of musicians brought together from 1966 onwards by the pianist Alexander von Schlippenbach (born 1938) in his "Globe Unity Orchestra": Albert Mangelsdorff (trombone, born 1928), Manfred Schoof (trumpet, born 1936), Peter Brötzmann (saxophone, born 1941), Gunter Hampel (vibraphone, bass clarinet, born 1937) etc.; also the "So-Called Left-Wing Radical Wind Orchestra" from Frankfurt/Main, formed round composer and pianist Heiner Goebbels in the seventies, and the groups centred on Berlin saxophonist Ernst-Ludwig Petrowsky, Dresden percussionist Günter Sommer and pianist Ulrich Gumpert from Jena.

This does not of course mean that the German jazz musicians had overtaken their American colleagues as regards their significance and contribution, even in their own country – this can be observed from the programmes of the Berlin Jazz Festival, the successor to the former Berlin Jazz Days. Apart from purely quantitative reasons, there are also cogent historical and musico-sociological reasons for this. They are still growing considerably stronger in the areas of rock and pop music, songs and musicals. Nevertheless, German rock music, once disparagingly referred to as "German Kraut Rock" or "Teutonic Noise Rock", has unexpectedly succeeded in achieving some international renown, for instance with the "Scorpions", who are also very well thought of in America and Britain. In particular, the musicians of the groups referred to as "New German Wave", such as "Interzone", "Einstürzende Neubauten", "Die Ärzte", the "Tote Hosen", the ludicrously primitive "Trio", later "Cosa Rosa", Heinz Rudolf Kunze, Philipp Boa and Katharina Franck were able to play and sing themselves free of the ambience of qualifying comparisons. In contrast to this, Udo Lindenberg (born 1946), with his predominantly German sung rock music, relies on a kind of casually enlightening show, and the musicians' group of "Tangerine Dream" (from 1967) on the sound seduction of their richly equipped electronics.

Perhaps, however, it was also as a counter-movement to the mechanical gear and bewildering glitter of lights that the simpler forms of presentation of the "Songmakers" received their special chance. This ranges, in a wide scattering of styles, from the commitment of the Bavarian Konstantin Wecker (born 1947) via Klaus Lage and the critical singers Hannes Wader and Franz Josef Degenhardt, to the actors Marius Müller-Westernhagen, Herbert Grönemeyer and Stefan Waggershausen.

Playing a special intermediate role between the two parts of Germany were those songmakers who, like Wolf Biermann, Bettina Wegener and Stephan Krawczyk had been expatriated from the GDR thanks to their critical attitude to the regime and found both freedom of opinion and also new stimulus for critical commitment in the Federal Republic.

The fact that, in contrast, average light music was hardly able to throw off its provincial character may be connected with some attributes, positive in themselves, of German musical life, which had a forestalling effect in this very particular: its stability and its socially rooted versatility, constantly regenerated from its own tradition. Pre-coined structures are present everywhere; and before anyone dared to plan a musical future in the altered circumstances in the years immediately following 1945, the old circumstances had already been reinstated in outline and in some of their fixed points. True, as a result of wartime destruction, there were at first few theatres, halls, teaching institutions, and many other things. But as soon as the basic necessities of life had been procured, *Länder,* communities, and private patrons began to convert – at least in the form of plans – their concepts of music and the transmission of music into architectural form. Once again proscenium stages appeared, with tiers of box and balcony seats in the auditorium; once again, towel-shaped concert halls – only the technical facilities on and behind the stage, as well as building materials, colour schemes, and formal decor were modernized to meet contemporary standards. But the chance of a fundamentally new design, drawing on different social conditions or new acoustic discoveries was scarcely ever exploited, with a few exceptions – for instance, the circular tiers of "vineyards" at the Philharmonia in Berlin by Hans Scharoun and the Neues Gewandhaus in Leipzig. Recently, however, we have learned from experience of the cultural centres that have come into being in London (Barbican) and Paris (Centre Pompidou) and have created similar institutions in Frankfurt am Main with the concert and congress centre "Alte Oper", in Cologne with the Philharmonie and in Munich with the "Gasteig". Nevertheless, the loving reconstruction of historic buildings still rules the day.

These "restorative" features in German musical life can be explained by its firmly rooted tradition; and the still astonishing density of publicly subsidized facilities is in turn based on that. Of the 80 or so towns with more than a hundred thousand inhabitants, only a quarter – mostly in conurbations – have no orchestra of their own. In comparison with foreign countries, the infrastructure of musical culture in Germany is generally impressive: some 70 music theatres, over 110 professional orchestras, far more than 700 music schools, hundreds of music festivals, military music corps, music libraries, music councils and other musical organizations, promotion of music in the context of foreign cultural policy, including the Goethe Institutes, public music archives, museums and musical memorials, municipal conservatories, choirs, promotion of music at resorts, colleges of music and training centres for musical professions ...

This high expenditure for a truly "wall-to-wall" promotion of concerts and opera has led to an abundant flowering of German musical life, with a lively exchange across frontiers. Top orchestras like the Berlin Philharmonic, the Dresden Staatskapelle and also the Munich Philharmonic, the Gewandhaus Orchestra in Leipzig, the Bamberg Symphonic and the radio orchestras have spread the reputation of an extremely active cultivation of music and a special orchestral culture in Germany, supported by a lively sense of sound, thanks to their many guest appearances on all five continents.

Conversely, the many festivals, which are usually the highlights of the German musical landscape during the summer months, are among the attractions for the wide influx of visitors from near and far: above all the Richard Wagner Festivals in Bayreuth, at which one is confronted with the work of the great musical dramatist more exclusively and directly than anywhere else; but also Mozart in Würzburg, Carl Maria von Weber in his native town of Eutin, Bach in Eisenach, Beethoven in Bonn, and Handel in Göttingen and Halle create motives for festivals – as does the general "Schleswig-Holstein Music Festival", scattered throughout that Federal *Land,* the Dresden Music Festivals and the Weimar Art Festival.

In view of this healthy picture, the worries of those responsible over the lack of young musical interpreters seem almost unfounded. Yet this problem does exist, and for years the "German Music Council", as the leading organization, has, with the support of the Federation, the *Länder* and the local authorities, taken effective measures against this in a pincer movement, as it were: the early recognition of talent and at the same time the animation of amateur music-making was promoted by means of the competition "Jugend musiziert" (youth makes music), while in the final stage of education, between the end of college and individual employment at concerts, the engagement agency programme known as the "Federal Selection of Concerts by Young Artists" stepped in and at the same time supplied the best way to manage the targeted award of grants for further study at master course level. A "German Music Competition" has recently been added to this, which, by means of prizes, aims to step up performance to the point of a chance of success at the "International Music Competition of the Broadcasting Corporations of the Federal Republic of Germany" in Munich.

The educational assistance and allocations thus given become early forms of the subvention culture. This, however – as an efficient and productive system – comes to absorb many of the unattached amateur impulses at the lower levels the more it becomes institutionalized at the highest levels; the force of momentum sets in. And thus the stabilizing subvention culture frequently becomes an impediment to the unaccustomed: active encouragement of New Music easily gets shifted onto the alibi territory of special events, and an opera première such as that of *Lear* by Aribert Reimann (born 1936) for the opening of the Munich Opera Festival is still the rare exception. For this very reason, the hardening of representative culture has long since conjured up a counter-movement of spontaneous music-making in squares and streets, in pedestrian precincts and subways. Amateur music, once to be found only in choral unions, wind instrument groups, or in the private sitting-room, is spreading. And it is undoubtedly to be welcomed if serious composers try to do justice to this development, not simply as Carl Orff (1895–1982) once did in *Schulwerk* by the simplification of instruments and musical scores, but by way of ambitious sound exercises using material without preconditions (voice, everyday articles) – as for instance Dieter Schnebel (born 1930) does. This is because a healthy musical life grows up from its base and requires the reactivating power of strong foundations just as much as the theoretical superstructure of the institutes of musical science in the Federal Republic of Germany, which, by the publication of complete editions – for instance of the works of Mozart, Hindemith, Schönberg, E. T. A. Hoffmann, Bach, Gluck, Beethoven and Richard Wagner – in association with publishers, in turn have an effect on the practice of music. Even Carl Maria von Weber, born in Schleswig-Holstein and active for many years in Dresden, who was described by Wagner as "the most German of all Germans", has now been accorded a complete critical edition. It seems that the last symptoms have vanished of that historical situation which has governed the cultural heritage of the Germans since the Second World War.

Wolfgang Sandner

The Munich Radio Orchestra and Jan Koetsier giving a concert in Schloss Herrenchiemsee, 1970.

Concert by the Bamberg Symphony Orchestra under Heinrich Hollreiser in Schloss Neuschwanstein, 1970.

The cultural centre at the Gasteig in Munich, which, besides the Philharmonia and the city's conservatory, houses two smaller concert halls, a library, and adult education facilities.

This rehearsal photograph from the Leipzig Gewandhaus unites three of the internationally best-known musicians of the former GDR: singers Theo Adam and Peter Schreier and the chief conductor of the Gewandhaus Orchestra, Kurt Masur, who since 1991 has also been director of the New York Philharmonic.

The Munich Philharmonic, conducted by Chief Music Director Sergiu Celibidache.

The competition of the Association of German Broadcasting Corporations (ARD), held annually for alternating solo instruments and chamber music instrumentation, is one of the internationally most respected music competitions. Illustration: the prize-winners in the clarinet section, 1987. Richard Rimbert (France), Anna-Maija Korsimaa (Finland), and Fabrizio Meloni (Italy).

The "International Holiday Courses for New Music", started by W. Steinecke, have been taking place in Darmstadt (Hesse) since 1946. Every year in concerts, seminars, and workshop talks, contemporary composers present their latest works for discussion.

Composer Hans Werner Henze, 1981, at the desk of the Cologne Radio Symphony Orchestra.

Karlheinz Stockhausen, 1977, as sound controller of his own works.

Conductor Michael Gielen (b. 1927), as director of the Frankfurt Opera from 1977 to 1987, helped modern director's theatre to break through on the operatic stage as well. Since the 87/88 season, he has been chief conductor of the South-West Radio Symphony Orchestra, Baden-Baden.

Bernd Alois Zimmermann (1918–70), an outsider among the important composers of the second half of the century, whose work is penetrating ever more strongly into the awareness of the musically interested public.

Since its scandal-wreathed première in Cologne in 1965, Bernd Alois Zimmermann's *The Soldiers* has succeeded in finding recognition as a masterpiece of modern opera to stand beside Schoenberg's *Moses and Aron* or Alban Berg's *Wozzeck.* Set from the Frankfurt production in 1981: producer Alfred Kirchner, stage by Karl Kneidl, musical direction by Michael Gielen.

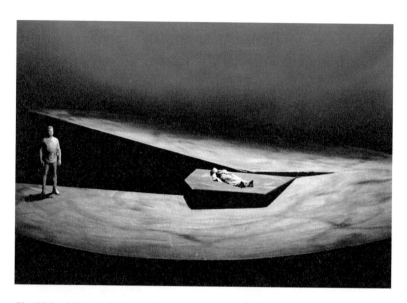

The Richard Wagner Festival, which takes place every summer in Bayreuth under the direction of Wagner's grandsons Wieland (1917–66) and Wolfgang (b. 1919), has developed from a place of pilgrimage to a workshop. Above: scene from the third act of *Siegfried* in Wolfgang Wagner's abstract, symbolic productions of 1975; below; striking visualization with the most up-to-date laser technology and masterly character direction in Harry Kupfer's *Rheingold* production 1988.

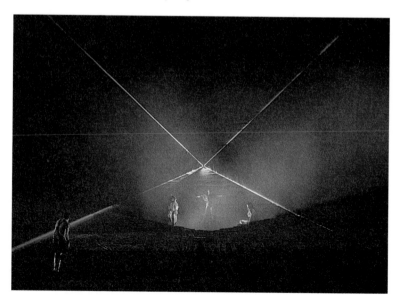

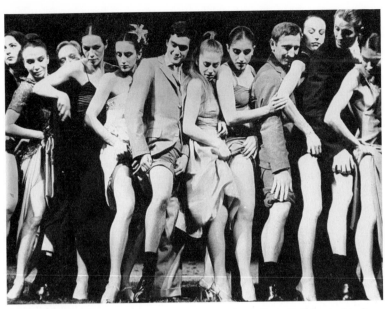

An independent theatrical form between dance, play and musical theatre has been created by the choreographer Pina Bausch since 1973 in Wuppertal: set photograph from *1980. A play by Pina Bausch.*

Paul Dessau composed the opera *Puntila* (1966) based on Bertolt Brecht's popular play *Herr Puntila und sein Knecht Matti*. Here is Reiner Süss in the title role in his "Dance on the Aquavit".

◀ Siegfried Matthus wrote his "Opera Vision" after Rainer Maria Rilke's *Die Weise von Liebe und Tod des Cornets Christoph Rilke* as a commissioned work for the reopening of the Semper Opera. Ruth Berghaus produced the première on 16 February 1985.

Musical pre-school education on so-called "Orff instruments", which are particularly easy for children to handle. With his "Schulwerk", the composer and dramatist Carl Orff created an integral educational concept on a musical base, which is now disseminated throughout the world.

In small towns, too, musical life is not only to be found on radio and television: pupils of the Youth Music School in Ditzingen (Baden-Württemberg) giving their fellow citizens a serenade evening.

The Zwinger, the baroque masterpiece of Pöppelmann and Permoser, built in 1710–32, provides the atmospheric framework for this summer open-air concert in Dresden.

Trombonist Albert Mangelsdorff (left, at the award ceremony of the Frankfurt Music Prize of 1986) is one of the styleforming German jazz musicians in the field of free jazz. Below: Mangelsdorff at a concert of the Berlin Jazz Days, 1971.

The Thad Jones/Mel Lewis Big Band at an appearance at the Munich jazz club ▶ "Domicile", 1978.

As in all areas of musical life, the broadcasting corporations under public law in the Federal Republic of Germany play an important role as promoters also in jazz – here for the Free-Jazz Days in Baden-Baden, supported by the Südwestfunk.

German song-makers: the national counterpart to the French chansonniers, the Anglo-American songwriters, the Italian cantatori. From above left: Konstantin Wecker, Hannes Wader, Herbert Grönemeyer, Franz Josef Degenhardt, Marius Müller-Westernhagen, and Wolf Biermann, an expatriate from the GDR since 1977.

Pop-rocker Udo Lindenberg was singing "The Special Train to Pankow" (right) years before re-unification.

The GDR group *Karat* stormed the hit parades in the East and West of divided Germany (centre) with "You have to cross Seven Bridges".

The shrillest voice in the pop scene of the Federal Republic: Nina Hagen (below).

A broad spectrum between "popular music" and genuine folk music has an audience of millions in the Federal Republic of Germany. Pictured above are the *Wildecker Herzbuben,* below is the folklore group *Oberschwankirchner Stubn- und Hausmusik.*

In summer the unjustly named "serious music" goes out into the country and into the open air. Above, the little town of Hitzacker on the Elbe, whose annual "Music Days" attract up to 10,000 visitors. Below, an open-air concert by the *Berlin Philharmonic Orchestra* on the "forest stage", where the same number of visitors is achieved at one blow.

There is an old tradition of musical instrument-making and organ-building in the Federal Republic of Germany. Besides manufacturing and repairing, the activity of the organ-builder includes tuning organs and harmoniums. Our picture shows the new organ – dedicated on 27 September, 1988 – in the historic church of St. Paul in Frankfurt/Main. It has three keyboards and pedals, 45 stops, mechanical play and stop action but also possesses additional electric stop action with 128 set combinations. It was built by the Bonn organ workshop Johannes Klais.

Arts and Crafts

Since the turn of the century, painters, sculptors, graphic artists, industrial designers, and the traditionalist craftsmen have played a considerable part in all spheres of purpose-oriented art. During the art-nouveau era, the designing artist and the executing craftsman were seldom identical. In the 20s, the "Bauhaus", on the other hand, encouraged not only the unity of all things artistic, but also a new, artistically independent activity of craftsmen. During the same period, the workshops of the town of Halle on Burg Giebichenstein gained still more importance, especially for the crafts. In the late 20s, "arts and crafts" had already assumed a respected position.

Their tradition remained alive even during the years from 1933 to 1945. After the end of the Second World War, many older artist-craftsmen, who had already been working before 1933 and had also received international awards after 1933, became the teachers of a younger generation.

The majority of the artists and craftsmen who had gone on working at the "Bauhaus" or at Burg Giebichenstein took up teaching posts in the West after 1945, or went to live and work there. Only a few remained in the former GDR. There the workshops of the town of Halle continued to function as a training centre, while the "Bauhaus" was long neglected. It was restored relatively late; nowadays there is a school of architecture in its premises, designed by Walter Gropius and excellently rebuilt.

Among the traditions on which the arts and crafts were able to build in the Federal Republic was the work of the "Deutscher Werkbund", which, in succession to William Morris, revived the idea of a new foundation of art on the basis of craftsmanship, with the determination to produce good industrial and commercial design. And yet the more the work of the *Werkbund* was directed towards industrial design, the more the arts and crafts seemed to be pushed to the fringes of developments. Nevertheless, the discontent with a certain uniformity in industrial mass production has been offering continuously increasing chances for the arts and crafts in recent decades.

The favourable conditions also included the rejection of the art-nouveau type of "arty handicraft" and a differentiation of disciplines. The "arty craftsman", who pursued anything and everything, was rightly mocked, while qualified potters, goldsmiths, glass and textile artists became more and more respected. The reaction to this development is reflected in many public and private collections, each devoted to one or the other of these disciplines. In accordance with the standards of their discipline, the greatest developments have been achieved in the collections of art ceramics, with glass and jewellery collections in second place.

The differentiation of the various kinds of arts and crafts corresponds to the differentiation of the artists. Individualism became the basis not only of painting and sculpture, but also of arts and crafts. However, the marked material orientation of arts and crafts led more rarely to that intellectualism which governed some trends in the fine arts. In many respects, the crafts have managed to catch up with the fine arts. Their products are no longer simply sold commercially but appear in exhibitions, museums, and galleries. Moreover, increasingly comprehensive catalogues are being produced on individual craftsmen or specific groups of artist-craftsmen; they are the basis of a growing, specialist literature on ceramics, glass, textiles, and goldsmith-ery.

The more distinctly artistic qualifications became pre-eminent over the ful-filment of functional tasks, the more the crafts came to converge with "free" art. The world of "objects", which had taken its place in the intermediate area between painting and sculpture, also made new developments possible in the traditional craft disciplines. These days, therefore, the crafts can scarcely be defined as aesthetically convincing functional art. Since the pur-pose-oriented demands are fulfilled largely by industrial production, and German industrial design is outstandingly accomplished especially in the areas of the home and everyday living, product design has ousted the crafts from many a curriculum in German art schools. Just recently there has been a growing realization in the schools as well that the crafts must regain importance, if design is not to lose contact with the real foundations of production. Federalism in the organization of cultural policy in the Federal Republic of Germany also has its effects on the crafts. In the "Association of German Arts and Crafts", the regional societies have joined together in an action body, which organizes national exhibitions at home and abroad, keeps up contacts with the World Organization for Arts and Crafts, and is active at fairs, with publications, and in public relations. The regional effort has also made it easier for artist-craftsmen to have direct contact with the public. The Government promotes the arts and crafts by means of awards such as the Hessian National Prize, which is awarded annually at the Frankfurt Fair, and the ceramics awards presented biennially by the *Land* of Rhineland-Palatinate. Parts of the prize money available are also allocated to artists who do not come from the Federal *Land* in question. Important, publicly esteemed awards of a regional character are also presented by the *Länder* North Rhine-Westphalia, Baden-Württemberg, Schleswig-Holstein and Hamburg, the last two with industry and associations involved as pa-trons.

Despite the regional orientation of cultural policy, which is based on the Constitution of the Federal Republic of Germany, there are few regional features in modern German crafts. Only where workshops work within an inherited tradition and have remained in the same place over decades – and even centuries – does their work reveal local or landscape-related character-istics. Essentially this still applies to a few folk-art potteries in Franconia, Bavaria, and the Middle-Rhine region.

Teachers who had worked in one place for a long time scarcely ever estab-lished a local "school". Almost without exception, the pupils chose to live away from the places where they had studied, not infrequently in the coun-tryside bordering on major cities. Consequently craftsmen of all disciplines are to be found all over the Federal Republic. The multiplicity of individual talents cannot easily be classified in stylistic categories. We shall name here only a few aspects and tendencies which seem particularly characteristic of German arts and crafts: "Bauhaus", *Werkbund,* and collaboration in indus-trial design have promoted rational, geometrically oriented developments, for instance in silverwork and ceramics. On the basis of scientific methodol-ogy, German ceramics achieved their internationally recognized level in glazes. Individualization encouraged free, artistic components, which dom-inate in jewellery, textile art, and glass. The criteria regarding aesthetics and craftmanship are remarkably strictly applied in the Federal Republic of Germany. Modern handicraft products have now become recognized col-lectors' objects for the museums, for instance in Berlin, Schleswig, Ham-burg, Bremen, Düsseldorf, Cologne, Frankfurt, Karlsruhe and Stuttgart.

The arts and crafts of the last four decades were collected in the museums of the former GDR – as in the West – but predominantly restricted to work from their own territory. The arts and crafts museums in Berlin-Köpenick, Leipzig and Dresden provide a good overview, while the museums in Erfurt and Weimar place their main emphasis on stocks of "Bauhaus" work.

Even before reunification, early contacts between craftsmen existed between the Western and Eastern Federal *Länder* through the organization of joint symposia and exhibitions. This development has intensified from 1990/91; the big international exhibition "Configura 1" in Erfurt in the early summer of 1991, which as well as works of "free" art included avant-garde crafts, demonstrated this, as did regional presentations such as the "Triennale of North German Arts and Crafts" in Schleswig in 1991 and Güstrow in 1992. Common features correspond to internationally observable developments, moving towards a free, more decoratively than functionally oriented form. There are still differences between West and East today in the Federal Re-public in the treatment of materials. The difficulty of obtaining the necessary material in the former GDR stimulated imagination, if the work in question allowed, especially in the area of tapestry and ceramics. It is to be expected that some inspiration will also emerge from this in the Western Federal *Länder*. This certainly applies to glass, the production of which in Thuringia is based on old traditions. In particular, the "blowing before the lamp" practised there (i.e. shaping over a gas flame) was and is a special achievement of German art glass-making.

Besides the topical aspects of arts and crafts, there is no doubt that work connected with the preservation of monuments will play a main role for a long time to come, the greater part of it by far in the new Federal *Länder,* whose building fabric has been neglected for decades. For the artistically oriented crafts, the reconstruction, faithful as regards both handicraft and style, of the internal fittings of the last nine centuries, as well as the addition of compartments in contemporary style, will present a challenge reaching into the next century.

Since the seventies more and more international exhibitions of arts and crafts have been organized. This trend, which takes account of and accompanies the growing European unification, will expand quantitatively and qualitatively to include the East European countries. Some arts and crafts disciplines will profit from this, especially the textile arts, through the Polish contributions, and glass-making through those of Czechoslovakia. Under such conditions, the arts and crafts, often wrongly declared dead, have an independent future alongside industrial design.

Heinz Spielmann

Ceramic objects in the border area between utilitarian vessel and free sculpture. Above: Ursula Scheid, "Bulbous Shape", 1986, porcelain, turned, striped decoration with slip containing iron and copper; stony, matt felspar glaze. Below left: Karl Scheid, "Flat Constructed Shape", 1987, porcelain, felspar glaze containing manganese and iron ore covering relief decoration; below right: Karl Scheid, "Flat Constructed Shape", 1988, porcelain, light felspar petalite glaze, linear decoration. Both artists live in Büdingen (Hesse).

Oberammergau
wood-carver
at work.

Wood sculpture and wood carving are crafts which have developed in Southern Germany in particular. From time immemorial, wooden sculptures of high quality have been created here, mainly on Christian themes.

During the work of weaving, the artist follows the tracing of her design cartoon stretched behind the warp threads. The step by step growth of the Gobelin can be recognized.

Rear view of a loom: details from bottom to top: two treadles for the reciprocal opening of the compartments (warp threads); cylinder on which the growing Gobelin is rolled up; behind this, the warp threads and tracing of the cartoon; above, the compartments and cylinder with the mounted warp threads.

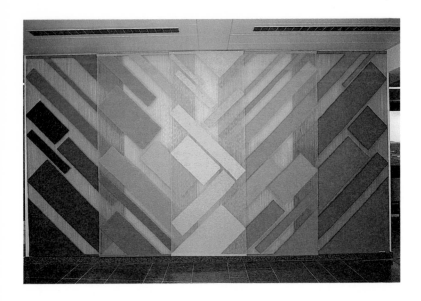

Most textile artists work to their own designs. We show here, as representative of many others, works by the Hamburg artist Anka Kröhnke which were made on commission within the "Art on Buildings" programme for the employment offices in Giessen (Hesse) and Munich. Above: "Contrary Spectrum", hemp-rope/cotton, 240 × 450 cm, 1987; below: "Inge", hemp-rope/cotton, twice 290 × 450 cm, 1985/86.

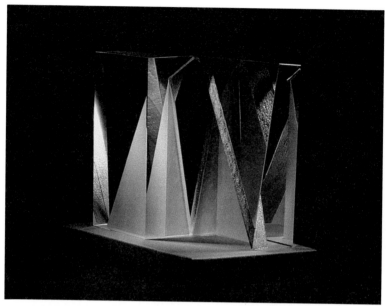

Willi Pistor, Hadamar (Hesse): "Glass Object", 1987, cut, 26 × 27 × 17 cm.

Ulrike Bahrs, Munich: "Turquoise Spiral", 1987, ebony, ruby glass, turquoise, silver, and gold.

Dörte Michaelis (b. 1957), "Bowl with slip painting", 1989: an example of ceramic development in the new Federal *Länder*.

A view of the *Länder*-wide "Triennale of North German Arts and Crafts" in the Schleswig-Holstein *Land* Museum Schloss Gottorf. Besides workshops from the region between Greifswald and Bremen, guests from Scandinavia were also represented in this exhibition.

Dagmar Lisske, "Tapestry from metal platelets", 1989/90. The artist, who lives in Greifswald, is among the craftworkers from Mecklenburg-Western Pomerania, who use the simplest materials to realize their work.

Isgard Moje-Wohlgemuth, Schwanewede near Bremen: "Glass Cylinder", 1988, height about 14.5 cm.

Antje Brüggemann, Bad Hersfeld (Hesse): "Tall Vessel with Blue Triangle", various mixtures, 1987; stoneware, about 38 cm high.

Founded in 1977, the Frankfurt Museum of Arts and Crafts was able, in April of 1985, to acquire this spectacular new building erected on the "Museum Bank" by the New York architect Richard Meier, whose origins are German. The museum's collections at present comprise about 30,000 objects and are divided up into four sections for European, East Asian, and Islamic art as well as book-making and calligraphy.

Founded in 1877, the Museum of Arts and Crafts in Hamburg is thus a full century older. Since then – almost without interruption – an annual show of the output of craftsmen from Northern Germany has taken place. The photograph shows an exhibition hall at the annual fair in 1987.

Gabriele Platt, Munich: "Without Title", wood, 1988, height ca. 200 cm

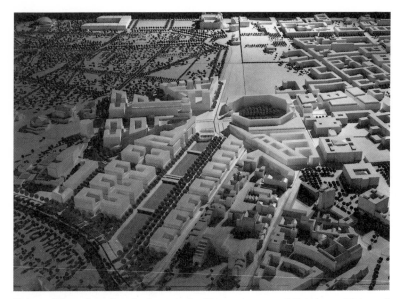

Future vision of modern business and office centre around Potsdamer Platz and Leipziger Platz in the core of Berlin, which had remained fallow building land through the devastation of the Second World War, the sector boundaries and finally the Wall (1961); above: the award-winning design by Heinz Hilmer and Christoph Sattler in the competition announced by the City Senate; on the horizon, one can see the Reichstag, under is the Brandenburg Gate and left from there Scharoun's Philharmonia; below: proposal by the Berlin architect Hans Kollhof from a workshop organized by the German Architectural Museum (Frankfurt), in which 21 national and international architectural teams took part. The concentration of high-rise blocks on the squares would simultaneously allow the rescue and restoration of the historic district between the Brandenburg Gate and the cathedral/Museumsinsel.

Architecture and the Preservation
of Historic Monuments

Architecture

After the Second World War, modern architecture in West Germany had great difficulty in finding a convincing new character of its own, since the tremendous destruction – some towns were in ruins to the tune of 80% of their buildings – initially enforced a form of reconstruction in which beauty was not considered; a roof over one's head was the most important thing.

The dictatorship of the National Socialists had had such a strong effect that no further attempt was made to link up again with the progressive tendencies in the German architecture of the 20s. As soon as economic conditions allowed, architects focused on the "international style", which came from the USA and later from Scandinavia as well to influence the new way of building in the rising Federal Republic.

Accordingly, scarcely anything that was built at that time had original strength and meaning. A typical example is the collection of unrelated adjacent residential buildings in the "Hansaviertel" in Berlin (West), which were designed by the then most famous architects in the world for the "Interbau 1957". These architects still believed in the clean-cut residential town amid greenery with tower-blocks in the park. Not urban 'spaces' were designed, but "surfaces" decorated in an arbitrarily formalistic way with high and low building typologies.

Moreover, the technically feasible also appeared as the desirable. The "car-friendly town" was not simply a theoretical model; it was not felt to be inhuman but quite natural to subject the town to traffic rather than the other way round. And the design principles adopted from America were handled more and more rigidly: Louis Sullivan's famous formula "form follows function" was, however, taken so literally that soon only function and no comprehensible, let alone unique form whatsoever was recognizable in architecture.

In accordance with this view that technical progress above all was the social motivating force, the architects Helmut Hentrich and Hubert Petschnigg designed the modern Düsseldorf symbol, the "Thyssen Tower-Block" (1960). Cool and elegant, self-assured and yet anonymous, these three slender glass panes, set in staggered parallel, signalize perfect, clear harmony: architecture without blemish, but also without soul.

How different, on the other hand, was the eruptive, contradictory, unfinished "Philharmonia" in Berlin (West) by Hans Scharoun (1963), which transformed music into architecture. The roofs have movement and the facades several faces at the same time; the hall resembles a vineyard, and the staircases are a spatial adventure. But the Philharmonia is a unique case. Only here could Scharoun, the champion of "organic building", realize his vision almost without compromise. Contemporary tendencies were running in a different direction, typified by the "Gallery of the 20th Century" in Berlin (West) by Ludwig Mies van der Rohe (1968), quite close to the Philharmonia: really no more than a noble, black, flat roof, supported by technically fascinating slender steel supports with mobile joints. The facade is so to speak "nothing", immaterial, merely glass. The extent to which Mies van der Rohe regarded this modern-classical temple of art as a work of art in itself is demonstrated by his contempt for its function, because he banned the actual museum into the cellars so that the purity of his creation should not be obscured by "contents". In this he preceded many post-modern architects.

For the time being, however, this building also remained a special case, because meanwhile German architects had discovered the "new brutalism" for themselves and were celebrating veritable orgies with plastically shaped concrete. Hundreds of new churches became more or less successful monuments to a new expressionism. This style reached its undisputed peak with Gottfried Böhm's townhall for Bensberg near Cologne (1964). The modern "fortress" lies like a crown on the heights of the little town. Movement becomes form. There is no longer any valid grid, and complicated rhythm, instead of a uniform beat, determines the arrangement of volumes and the subdivision of facades.

In perverted form, concrete brutalism has in its day become accepted even for residential buildings: for instance, the planners of the "Märkische Viertel" (1965) in Berlin (West) piled up sheer mountains of residences, with jagged silhouettes up to the twenty-second floor, quite without reference to the real requirements of the people "accommodated" there, who would really prefer to live close to the earth, below the treetops. Criticism of the Märkische Viertel brought a change of trend: people began to remember the long scorned form of living round courtyards and the spatial effect of streets enclosed on both sides (the Steilshoop Settlement in Hamburg; later on the well designed blocks of flats in Karlsruhe or Munich by Heinz Hilmer and Christoph Sattler). Even the very low-rise but clustered form of housing came into play again (Volkardey Residential Park in Ratingen by Peter Volkamer and Franz Wetzel, 1974).

Apart from these general tendencies in the 70s, there were of course always individual achievements in West German architecture, which either triggered further developments and imitations or remained admired exceptions: for instance, the "four-cylinder" suspension tower-building for the "Bayerische Motorenwerke" BMW in Munich by Karl Schwanzer (1972), the cheerful tent architecture with the swinging cable roofs over the Olympic Park in Munich by Günter Behnisch and Partners (1967/72, based on the experience of Frei Otto), Egon Eiermann's "office goblets", for Olivetti in Frankfurt (1972), the precisely cut composition of goldglass office-block prisms for the administration of the German Health Insurance in Cologne by F. W. Kraemer, Günter Pfennig, and Ernst Sieverts (1970), and the graceful, transparent school buildings, again by G. Behnisch and Partners (Lorch, 1973; Dachau, 1975; Rothenburg, 1979; School for mentally disabled children in Bad Rappenau, 1987–1991), as well as the artistically well planned sections of Constance University campus by Eugen Schneble and W. von Wolff (1972), and the science buildings by Hermann Fehling and Daniel Gogel, the main representatives of organic architecture after H. Scharoun (Max-Planck Institutes of Education in Berlin, 1965–1974, and for Astrophysics in Garching near Munich, 1975–1979, as well as the extension of the Meteorological Institute at the Free University of Berlin 1991).

In the 80s, the scene was set for everyone to experience the late-capitalist "anything goes" attitude in architecture. Many are the forms invented by the architect as "Homo Ludens" in his striving for the "reintroduction of the past into the present" (Johannes Berger). Neo-rationalists – influenced by the Italian Aldo Rossi or the Spaniard Ricardo Bofill – compose, from historical "type elements" or archetypical forms (pillars, portals, temple gables, stoa, rotunda, campanile), ever new "ensembles" for commerce and trade, culture, education, or leisure, even for residential clusters; the contents are often interchangeable. Other post-modern architects – just like stage designers or creators of fashion – cover old and new buildings with a decor which recalls the eclecticism of the founding period, the "art nouveau" movement and the Viennese Secession. Even high-rises were not exempt from this mania.

The museum as a treasure chest of the past moves as though by its own volition to the centre stage of the postmodern building event. Lying hidden in cellars or brought to light during archaeological excavations, the varied collections of culture conscious patrons – they all need space to be ready for the leisure society. Here design, choice of materials, and concept of display go to extremes: from Munich's Neue Pinakothek (New Picture Gallery) with its compact, castle-like, foreboding exterior forms and the traditional bourgeois way of presenting 19th-century art in a sequence of solemn interiors (Alexander von Branca, 1967–1985) to the Abteiberg City Museum in Mönchengladbach (Rhineland) with its complexity of forms which, however, follows an inner logic similar to that of a collage. For each object in the collection (works from the expressionists to the present) an appropriate architectonic environment was created (designed by Hans Hollein, Vienna, in close cooperation with museum curator Johannes Cladders, 1972–1982). As impressive proof also of its leading role in culture management, the economic metropolis of Frankfurt am Main features 13 museum buildings. On the Schaumainkai, among others are being developed the German Architectural Museum (O.M. Ungers, 1981–1984), the Museum of Arts and Crafts (Richard Meier, New York, 1982–1985) and the new Municipal Gallery of the Städel Art Institute (Gustav Peichl, Vienna, 1989–1991). On the other side of the Main, right in the heart of the old town, J.P. Kleihues has revived the ruins of the Carmelite monastery into the Museum of Pre- and Early History (1985–1989); the Schirn Art Hall (D. Bangert, Jansen, Scholz & Schultes, 1983–1985) and a row of townhouses – like an open-air architectural gallery – is placed between the cathedral and the Römer town hall; northwards, on a three-cornered remnant of a lot, Hans Hollein has inserted the Museum of Modern Art (1987–1991), the splendid facades of which will outstrip the others.

In the meantime, however, the spectacular museum buildings are overshadowed by a ring of new high-rise blocks: "Building culture and Commerce" visions of a postmodern skyline on the American pattern are becoming bolder and bolder! O.M. Unger's "Torhaus" at the exhibition centre shows the way – his vast window on the world became overnight the eloquent international symbol of the city; Helmut Jahn's "Campanile" (256 metres high) and the "Emperor's Crown" by Kohn/Pederson/Fox on the edge of the West End continue this trend.

Unlike Frankfurt am Main, West Berlin was designated a location for innovative architecture "from above" as it were, through the International Building Exhibition (IBA) 1984–1987. Architects from all over the world, young and old, had the chance to translate into practice their ideas for "city repair", for a new urban quality of life: inside the IBA-old under the direction of H.-W. Hämer (models for careful urban rehabilitation in Kreuzberg with the participation of those concerned) and inside the IBA-new under the direction of J.P. Kleihues (reconstruction of built round squares and closed street fronts, designs for "town villas"). Further "solitaires" came into being in the meantime near the National Gallery and the Philharmonia, unrelated to one another, surrounded by greenery, fenced round or resurfaced, like the Science Centre by J. Stirling (1984–1987) and – according to designs by the long-dead masters – the Bauhausarchiv (Walter Gropius, 1976–1978), the State Library and the Chamber Music Hall (H. Scharoun, 1967–1978, 1984–1987 respectively).

Compared to such architectural and artistic highlights, the initiatives to advance ecological or participatory ways of building and to apply appropriate construction techniques and materials appear rather modest. Yet precisely these initiatives would deserve increased support nowadays as being part of a comprehensive strategy to preserve natural resources. Of a model character is the "Emscher Park" of the International Building Exhibition (1988–1999, directed by K. Ganser and P. Zlonicky): it concerns a structure programme of North Rhine-Westphalia member-state and the 17 towns in the northern Ruhr area, a "Workshop for the Renovation of an Industrial Region" with seven fields of work or pilot projects encompassing 70 individual projects (affecting 500 hectares). The first results are expected in 1994.

How differently on the other hand did architecture and urban development proceed in the GDR! The models came from Moscow and prescribed a national form with socialist content; un-national forms were not possible, that is to say above all the International Style as a perfect example of western decadence. With the national cultural heritage as their base, architects and urban planners in the GDR had to strive for an architectural form which would be understood by the people and correspond to their particularity and sense of beauty (Handbook of Architecture 1954). The socialist content had to underline the superiority of socialism over capitalism in terms of building form. Beauty, shine and monumentality seemed the means to an end. The Reconstruction Act (September 1950) afforded the state a free hand over building land. Vast new order projects, which West German planners would never dare dream of undertaking, were possible in principle. Le Corbusier's requirements for a division of the functions of living, work, recreation and transport (Charter of Athens, 1933) were incorporated in diluted form in the "16 Principles of City Building" (1950), which together with the "Principles of Planning and Design of Socialist City Centres" of the German Building Academy (1960) set out the guidelines of the construction industry in the GDR: dominating community buildings (concise and emotionally effective high-rise structures) on large squares for parades and celebrations constitute the city centre, from which the main arteries, lined with representative blocks of flats, lead to the production plants. Four new towns for the workers of large industrial combines offered the first opportunities to translate theory into practice: Eisenhüttenstadt (plans by Kurt W. Leucht, 1951, borrowed from the Baroque art of city building, first planned for 30,000 inhabitants, finally for 110,000 inhabitants up to the year 2000); Hoyerswerda (planned by the State Design Office of Urban and Rural Planning Halle from 1954, carried out from the outset with an industrial prefabrication method of construction, 47,000 inhabitants in 1967); Schwedt/Oder, which emerged on the site of a town destroyed in the Second World War (according to an idea by S. Selmanagic from 1960, for 14,000 inhabitants) and Halle/Neustadt (likewise designed by the State Planning Office Halle from 1960, for 70,000 inhabitants up to 1973).

Quite in the spirit of these "Principles" is the extension of the Frankfurter
Allee (Stalin Allee) in East Berlin; adjoining residential areas on both sides
had suffered greatly in the war. There have been plans for an East-West-
axis since 1920; they are taken up in Hans Scharoun's proposal for a city
based on a ribbon development with community units for 4,000 to 5,000
inhabitants, even the apartment types originated from the socially aware
architects of the 1920s (B. Taut, M. Wagner, W. Gropius, Ernst May). The
"Wohnzelle Berlin-Friedrichshain" (1949, planned also by Scharoun) and
the nine-storied "High-rise Building on the Weberwiese" by Hermann
Henselmann of the Corbusier school (1951–1952, and protected since 1975)
begin this trend. After there are the stretches between Strausberger Platz
and Frankfurter Tor (planning and implementation under the direction of
H. Henselmann, 1949–1960). The street space was widened to 90 metres,
underneath runs the tube, dominating high structures were established: with
the staggered building volumes "Haus Berlin" and "Haus des Kindes", on
Strausberger Platz (1951–1953) Henselmann takes up Bruno Möhring's
blueprint for high-rise construction from 1920; whereas with his tower
building on the Frankfurter Tor (1957–1961), he harks back to everybody's
trusted symbols of national architecture, Gontard's domed towers (1780) on
the Gendarmenmarkt. Indeed for the time being, this stretch of the Stalin-
Allee has remained like a torso. One reason for this was that competitions
for the "Central Axis of the Capital of the GDR", e. g. 1958/59 with the
participation of 56 authors' collectives, yielded no convincing urban spatial
ideas for arranging the 3600 metre-long stretch from the Brandenburg Gate
over August-Bebel-Platz, the "central district" with the Palace of the Republic (Heinz Graffunder and K.-E. Swora, 1973–1976) to Alexander Platz.
The situation today has developed from continually altered section plans.
Even the building-up of the central squares and main arteries in the regional
capitals (for example, the Altmarkt in Dresden, the Rossmarkt in Leipzig
or the Lange Strasse in Rostock) was dragging reluctantly along. Twenty-
five years elapsed until Heldenplatz in the exhibition town of Leipzig received its structural setting: by way of the Opera House (1956–1960), the
dominant of the university skyscraper (collective H. Siegel/Gross/Ullmann
in collaboration with H. Henselmann, 1968–1973, 142 metres high) and the
New Concert Hall (urban concept H. Siegel, 1977–1981).
More and more, architecture and urban planning underlay the state planned
economy. By standardization, industrial prefabrication not only restricted
possible variations in ground plans, arrangement and design of buildings,
but also limited potential groups of applicants for competitions. One kept
oneself to oneself. Monotony, emptiness, distance spread everywhere, in the
continuing extension of the Stalin Allee as well as in the new towns on
which the building potential was concentrating. Attempts at a more flexible

type of prefabricated panelled building in the old towns, similar at least in decor to local traditions, finally begin in the middle of the 1970s: they range from the still stereotyped city block system in Greifswald to the almost elegant Five gabled house of the "Industrial housing type series 83" on University Square in Rostock.

Despite all the differences there were similarities in German-German building: in the GDR, industrial architecture remained a refuge for functionalist building right up to the 1970s; buildings in the "Stile nuovo" with fluid space, elegant hanging staircases, furnished with cone-shaped lamps and kidney-shaped tables, were being produced to the beginning of the 1960s in both the East and West. Regional architecture also lived on in many places in the provinces; this architecture could easily be interpreted as "national". Perhaps their later products are the "true to the original" reconstructed historic quarters and rows of houses for comfort and not "void of memory" (Umberto Eco) around the Nikolaikirche in East Berlin or in front of the Römer old town hall in Frankfurt am Main.

What will the common architecture of the future look like? Does H.-W. Hämer rightly fear an "all-German prefabricated panelled type", i.e., old town rehabilitation on the West German model of the 1960s brought about by pressure and haste from the construction industry, without prospects and without incorporating the experiences of Kreuzberg (West Berlin) and Prenzlauer Berg (East Berlin)? What will happen to the unified centre of Berlin?

Peter M. Bode / Ingrid Brock

The Thyssen Tower-Block in Düsseldorf (1960): Architects: Helmut Hentrich, Hubert Petschnigg and colleagues.

◀ Hans Scharoun's Philharmonia (1960 to 1963, in the background) and Chamber Music Hall (1984–1987, posthumously carried out by his pupil Edgar Wisniewski) in the Tiergarten area represent the most important complex of organic building in Germany.

◀ The town hall of Bensberg near Cologne (North Rhine-Westphalia) represents a climax in the architecture of "New Brutalism" in the Federal Republic of Germany. The modern crest of the town is raised on the wall remains of the old castle: it seems almost too massive for the little half-timbered town at its feet. Architect: Gottfried Böhm, 1964–67.

The new Science Centre in Berlin: stoa, amphitheatre, campanile, and church are conjured up by the British architect James Stirling in the complex, completed in 1988, in the Tiergarten district. The right side of the photo shows the "Gallery of the 20th Century" by Ludwig Mies van der Rohe (1968).

Hermann Henselmann stresses the two squares, which delineate the first segment of the Frankfurter Allee (Stalin Allee) in East Berlin; in the picture, the "Haus des Kindes" on Strausberger Platz, which is still oriented towards the high-rise building of the 1920s (H. Henselmann, R. Göpfert, E. Leibold, 1951–53); the circular fountains (30 metres in diameter) were designed by Achim Kühn, H. Graffunder and R. Rühle (1967).

The satellite town "Märkisches Viertel" in Berlin (West), built 1965–1970 by various architectural bureaux at home and abroad in accordance with an urban development plan by Senate Building Director Düttmann. The number of floors and hence the density of population were increased at a later stage: this impaired the quality of life and gave rise to criticism.

City repair in West Berlin as a result of the International Building Exhibition (IBA) in the 1980s: new building development between the Lützowufer and Lützowplatz by the Tessin architect Mario Botta (corner house) and (immediately on the right) by the English architects Peter Cook and Christine Hawley.

The Five gabled house on the University Square in Rostock (placed between two corner houses), one of the few examples that shows that with imagination and thought in arranging facades even types of prefabricated panelled building could generate impressive architecture; use: shops on the ground floor, 143 flats of different sizes in the upper 6 floors (Authorcollective WBK Rostock, KB FPT; design: Peter Baumbach, J. Deutler, 1983).

Frankfurt/Main: view from the cathedral tower over the southern Römerberg with a row of postmodern town houses in the Saalgasse and the modest, functional residential buildings of the earliest postwar period. Beyond the Main, the so-called "Museum Bank" on the Schaumainkai (the photograph links up with the photograph opposite).

One of the most famous postmodern buildings is O. Unger's Turmhaus (Tower House) on the exhibition centre in Frankfurt/Main (built 1984–87, 117 metres high). The catchy combination of crystal squares and the gigantic red sandstone arched opening made it the international symbol of the city overnight.

Frankfurt/Main: view of the city from the cathedral tower across the western Römerberg. Left foreground: rotunda of the Kulturschirn (architects D. Bangert, Jansen, Scholz & Schultes, 1987); on the right, Technical City Hall (Bartsch, Thürwächter, Weber, 1972); in the centre, the gabled houses of the Römer historic town hall, repaired after war damage, and the Paulskirche (the church of St. Paul: new interior by Schwarz and Krahn, 1949). A ring of high-rise buildings characterizes the skyline from the Main to the Exhibition Centre/West End.

Based on the model of Hans Scharoun's Berlin Philharmonia, without attaining its rigour and vibrant ease, is the concert hall of the new Leipzig Gewandhaus, which was opened on the 8 October, 1981. Architects: Rudolf Skoda and Volker Sieg.

"High dominant" of the Leipzig cityscape is the 142 metre-high University Tower, which was erected on the site of the Universitätskirche (University church) blown away in 1968, and the worn away remains of the main building of the old University.

Architecture as the symbolization of democratic institutions: the new building for the North Rhine-Westphalian Parliament in Düsseldorf, opened in the autumn of 1988, presents the plenary chamber as the sun encircled by the rooms for the parties and committees as though by planets. The outer circle segments house the offices of the members of parliament. Architects: Fritz Eller and Partners.

Joint Technical Production Centre (Institute of machine tools and manufacturing technology of the Technical University, and Fraunhofer Institute of production plants and construction techniques) on the bend of the Spree in Berlin, designed by Gerd Fesel and Peter Bayerer (1982–1986): around the test area (3200 sq. metres) in the large, round hall there are office space, workrooms, laboratories and computer equipment.

One of the most significant high-rise office buildings of the 1970s was built on the edge of the Olympic grounds in Munich in accordance with the plans of the Austrian architect Karl Schwanzer (1972) in order to house the administration of the Bavarian car manufacturer BMW.

Two energy-saving houses in Tübingen (Baden-Württemberg): highly retaining walls ▶ made of Ytong brick, optimized roof slopes, and the greenhouse effect of the glass section attached to the south front allow solar energy to be used so effectively that the cost for additional heating per house and year amounts to only 500 DM (1986); project by LOG ID Grüne Solararchitektur, D. Schempp, 1985.

View across Munich's Olympic Park, with swimming stadium and Olympic hall under the tent roof in the foreground, the great Olympic stadium and the cycle stadium to the left in the background. Overall planning for the Olympic Games of 1972 and tent-roof construction by architects G. Behnisch & Partners, 1967–1972.

School for the mentally disabled in Bad Rappenau near Stuttgart (1987–1991): in keeping with modern educational ideas, architects G. Behnisch & Partners transformed the inner space into a protected outer space.

Transport architecture reached a notable level in postwar Germany, particularly in bridge-building where not only technical and constructive but also outstanding architectonic solutions were found, as the aerial photograph of Cologne on the Rhine shows: in the lower part of the picture the Severinsbrücke; on the right hand side of the river, the bridge is suspended by sloping cables on its asymmetrical pylon, the main span comes to 302 metres (engineer Fritz Leonhardt and architect Gerd Lohmer, 1959); in the centre, the Deutzer Rheinbrücke (builder: Fritz Leonhardt 1947–48), and in the background the Hohenzollernbrücke, which was the first railway connection over the Rhine (original design in 1859).

The illustration underneath shows the pylon and suspension cables of the Severinsbrücke in detail.

Gottfried Semper's second Dresden Hoftheater (1871 to 1878) suffered heavy damage in the Second World War. After extensive safeguarding work 1952–57 (in accordance with the reports by engineers Walter Henn and Wolfgang Preiss), the reconstruction of the State Opera began from 1965; the opera could be reopened on the 40th anniversary of the destruction (13 February, 1985) following careful restoration and amendments of the interior decoration. Above, a general view of the Opera, below on the left, a view of one of the upper vestibules (state of conservation, 1982).

Preservation of Historic Monuments

After the Second World War, the preservation of historic monuments in the Federal Republic of Germany was faced with almost insuperable tasks, given the paucity of funds then available. First of all, difficult safety measures on almost all the important cathedrals and churches in the bombed cities had to be carried out, followed by extensive reconstruction. On this occasion, an earlier version, regarded as more valuable, was often made, like the Romanesque churches in Cologne or at St. Michael in Hildesheim.

In the towns of the former GDR with their numerous church ruins, the Second World War still seems close. On its own, its poor safeguarding lacked strength in the past decades. Still splendid but heavily damaged is the Georgenkirche (church of St. George) in Wismar (Mecklenburg), which towers as ever above the old East sea town. Other church ruins in the East as well as the West were preserved as memorial and commemorative places, like the Marienkirche (church of St. Mary) in Frankfurt/Oder, the Franciscan church in East Berlin, parts of the Kaiser-Wilhelm-Gedächtniskirche (Emperor William Remembrance Church) in West Berlin, the long nave of the Barfüsserkirche (church of the Barefooted monastic order) in Erfurt (Thuringia) or St. Katherinen (church of St. Katherine) in Nuremberg.

Secular buildings were more often subjected to far-reaching alterations: their interiors were divided up in a completely new way (Hanover Opera House), or destroyed sections were erected in modern styles (Germanic National Museum, Nuremberg; the Leinenschloss in Hanover as the state parliament of Lower Saxony). Important buildings in the East experienced even more thorough treatment, even when they had not been damaged in the war, especially castles and manor houses: if they were inappropriate for charitable purposes, they were simply plundered and demolished. An overall view of the damaged cultural property lost is still to be compiled. Indeed, in Saxony alone, 129 out of 397 castles and manor houses under preservation were lost in this way in the immediate postwar period (as of 1948).

Even the rehabilitation of destroyed city centres did not always link up with tradition. Examples of reconstructions according to old plans – such as the principal market square in Münster – or of the preservation of the historic town structure with its street network and building lines, with characteristic roof shapes and local building materials – such as in the reconstruction of Nuremberg – are rare. On the contrary, the majority of the local buildings and planning authorities seized the opportunity for urban redevelopment; the plans for Hanover by Rudolf Hillebrecht were considered a model in their day.

In East Germany, rebuilding started on a large scale between 1955 and 1970, however now with an ideologically motivated programme of urban development that did not consider historically evolved city structures or traditional architectonic-urban landmarks: not just heavily damaged, but also lightly affected monuments were cleared away. The public only came to know about the destruction of the town castles of Potsdam and Berlin, perhaps also about the Garnisonkirche (the Garnison church). However, that the Marienkirche (church of St. Mary) in Wismar, the Jacobikirche (church of St. Jacob) in Rostock, several churches in Magdeburg, the University-church, St. Matthias and St. John churches in Leipzig, the Sophienkirche (church of St. Sophie) and a further 13 church ruins in Dresden – to quote just a few examples – fell victim to this mania, has long been forgotten, not to mention the quite recuperable town houses and palais in Dresden, Leipzig, Magdeburg or Potsdam.

Today, in the last ten years of the century, the tasks of monument conservation have not diminished; on the contrary a number of new fields of activity have arisen.

Now as before, concern for the outstanding monuments absorbs the greater part of the expert services. This is no longer by any means a case of ordinary building maintenance against wear and tear, or of simple protective measures against damage; it now involves the development of modern conservation methods of a chemical, physical, and constructive nature against accelerated processes of deterioration brought about, for instance, by increased air pollution, the use of old materials and improper building stuffs in the postwar period or by the vibration of street and air traffic. The solution of such problems (stone conservation, wood protection, strengthening of wall masonry, consolidating foundations, installing protective glazing for medieval stained-glass windows) requires close cooperation with scientific and technological disciplines. A number of specialized institutions came into being which can already fall back on a wealth of experience. Besides workshops for the restoration of moveable works of art, some regional monument offices maintain their own research facilities – an example is the Bavarian Regional Office with its central laboratory for stone conservation in Schloss Seehof near Bamberg or the monument offices of Hesse, Rhineland-Palatinate and Saarland with the Institute for Stone Conservation in Wiesbaden.

The constantly increasing restoration work on the major religious buildings is carried out or coordinated by on-site shops and church conservation offices. This type of work is seen at its most extensive at Cologne Cathedral: the poor-quality sandstone used to complete the cathedral in the 19th century has not stopped crumbling; its replacement by more resistant basalt lava here approaches the level of gradual rebuilding of the cathedral.

The question of the care and use of churches and monasteries in the GDR was far more urgent. With the setting up of construction teams specific to churches, one sought to rectify the shortage of building contractors, and furthermore to protect the continued existence of worship and church activities in the face of increasing secularization. However, it was not uncommon that the installation of small heated Winterkirchen (winter churches) and parish centres interfered with the historic substance and perception of space. Adaptive uses for churches – not just in the East – were particularly fraught with problems (the Oceanographic Museum in the Nikolaikirche in Rostock, the old people's home in the Paulinerkirche in Hildesheim).

As exemplary measures regarding moveable works of art, we can point to the restoration of the "Angelic Greeting" by Veit Stoss in the Nuremberg Church of St. Lawrence for the Dürer Year 1971 and the "Triumphal Cross Group" by Bernt Notke in Lübeck Cathedral. The decisions on conservation measures were based on the results of a systematic study of the origins and history of these polychrome wooden sculptures; the work on both was carried out in an *ad hoc* workshop, supervised by an international team of experts. In the GDR, the majority of art works of this type lacked regular care: today, they are not only threatened by degradation but also by theft and vandalism; examples include the hundreds of preserved wing-altars or the provisionally stored fittings which could only be rescued at the last minute from churches earmarked for demolition.

Careful preparation and planning are also necessary in the restoration of historic interiors in churches and monasteries, castles and town halls. Earlier conversions and frequent overpainting of frescoes often render decisions for specific interior decoration setting difficult. Aesthetic aspects and those which constitute historical documentation have to be considered equally. The pilgrimage church in the Wies near Steingaden in the "Pfaffenwinkel", a jewel of the bright southern German Rococo, glitters anew after a 7-year long intervention by 80 specialists. Exemplary interior restorations have also been carried out recently at Augsburg Cathedral (1981–1987), at Doberan Minster (Mecklenburg) and in the Annenkirche (church of St. Anne) in Annaberg (Saxony) – to name just a few examples.

Among the most exacting projects of monument preservation are the restoration of important castles, gardens, and landscape ensembles and their interiors – many are of worldwide importance like the memorials of classical German literature in Weimar, the Dessau/Wörlitz parks in Saxony-Anhalt, the residences and gardens of Augustusburg and Falkenlust in Brühl am Rhein and above all the parks of Berlin-Potsdam with the Glienicke Hunting Lodge, the Island of Peacocks and Sanssouci, which now feature – like the residences in Brühl – on UNESCO's List of World Cultural Heritage.

The protection of authentic village structures and early suburban and rural workers' housing estates appears particularly difficult in the modern service-oriented society. Owing to increased urbanisation and the restructuring of industry and agriculture, open-cast coal mining etc., records of the life, work and culture of entire sections of the population are at risk of being wiped out altogether. Local history museums and open-air museums can take on only a selection of objects, and can hardly be expected to document contexts of social and economic history, much less landscape. An impression of comprehensive folk art touching on all areas of life is still conveyed by the beautiful weaving villages in the Oberlausitz, certain half-timbered villages in Thuringia, Hesse and Franconia, low-German hall-type farmhouses or the Spreewalddorf (Spree Forest village) Lehde near Berlin. A new branch of monument preservation arose with the protection accorded to technical monuments and the collection of records of industrial culture. Early functional buildings such as machine shops, water towers, mining plants are especially threatened by dilapidation and demolition as their specific use-oriented construction means that they can only be adapted to modern methods of production or new functions with great difficulty. Even the many once spectacular civil transport structures are no longer capable of meeting present-day requirements and finally have to give way to new constructions on the same site.

The main challenge of monument conservation is still that of urban preservation and the protection of sites. During the first wave of West German building euphoria in the 1960s, hundreds of communes whose old centres had survived the war without major damage, e. g., Erlangen, Reutlingen or Itzehoe – just to mark out the geographical areas – followed modern concepts of urban renewal: they consisted of the dispersal of the old city centres for the building of department stores, banks, insurance offices and public administration, and a correspondingly extended system for traffic. This one-sided concentration of new functions led to the depopulation of inner city areas, a situation which cannot even be concealed by the generously conceived pedestrian precincts. Ultimately, countermovements sprang up: in many instances, the citizens who were directly affected by speculative operations took the initiative. However, the European Heritage Year 1975 marked the start of a general change in restoration policy.

In the historic towns of the GDR, renovation took on an even more radical shape, even though urban sites were grounded in its Monument Protection Act and specialized institutes had produced considerable preliminary work through "urban development analyses" (with charts and description of monument value): whole inner-city areas had to make space for "culture palaces" as in Erfurt recently; main arteries and parade squares broke up the historic outline of the town. On the other hand, the decline of the city centres spared by the war was simply precipitated by an inappropriate social and property policy, inadequate building maintenance and a criminally neglected supply and waste management network. This occurred to such an extent that there is hardly any chance of conserving their authentic substance. Only 20 years ago, Leipzig was perhaps one of the best conserved 19th-century German cities; today, one wanders through a crumbling half-ruined landscape with gaping holes. Finally, even monument curators suggested replacing whole areas by erecting prefabricated constructions on the historic layout of blocks: examples of this can be seen in Greifswald and Cottbus, Halle and Rostock.

Many initiatives for safeguarding architectural heritage were developed after Reunification: an immediate special programme on the lines of the West German "Pilot Projects" of the European Heritage Year in Alsfeld, Berlin (Kreuzberg), Rothenburg ob der Tauber, Trier, Xanten – then extended to Bamberg, Lübeck and Regensburg – should now afford swift aid to Brandenburg, Halberstadt, Meissen, Stralsund, and Weimar, meanwhile, the "Assistance Programme for Monument Protection" of the Federal Ministry of Construction encompasses 80 towns in the new member states. Further more object-oriented assistance will be achieved through partnerships at the federal and local levels, by donations and technical exchanges of experience.

On principle, one should stress: the preservation of urban living space with its multiplicity of functions and human-oriented scale cannot only be the task of those affected or those concerned with the preservation of monuments, but must become the concern of the whole community and enter into its planning. Naturally it is not possible to apply the same principles to urban conservation as to the restoration of individual monuments. The preservation of structural features and housing typologies should remain to the fore, even when historic substance is replaced by new buildings.

A particular problem of heritage protection which touches on basic questions of the public's understanding of historic monuments, is demonstrated in the reconstruction of historic monuments that were completely destroyed in the war or lost due to other factors in the postwar period, as they have been discussed anew since Reunification, e. g., the Frauenkirche in Dresden, which has been lying in ruins since the bombing of 13 February, 1945. The Association of State Monument Conservators of the Federal Republic of Germany addressed itself to this complex of questions at its Annual Meeting in Potsdam, 11 June 1991 in a statement quoted in verbatim on account of its fundamental importance: "Like all Germans, the state monument conservators remember with sadness the losses of important historic monuments as a consequence of the Second World War and the ensuing political decisions not only in the German Democratic Republic, but also in the Federal Republic of Germany. They express the understanding of the desire to recover destroyed architectural work by building copies. Indeed, they emphatically point out that this wish cannot be fulfilled. The importance of historic monuments as evidence of great past achievements does not solely reside in the artistic ideas that embody them, but rather in their form, conditioned by time, materials and art with all their traces of fortune. Like history itself, the inherited material form is irrepeatable as a record of history. Therefore the reproduction of lost historic monuments can only be significant as a present action. In no event can copies ever be historic monuments because the latter recall great achievements of the past and keep alive memories of the historical process with its ups and downs. Monument conservators are only committed to non-reproduced testimonies of history and have to warn when memories in public spaces are possibly threatened with deletion."

The Preservation of Monuments in the Federal Republic of Germany comes under the independent cultural authority of the *Länder* (member states). After the Second World War, the *Länder* passed new legislation of historic preservation, adapted to the broader concept of the monument. The authorities responsible are the Regional Monument Offices or Regional Curators. Many cities with a significant building heritage also run their own local monument offices or appropriate sections in their building or cultural authorities. Cathedral workshops and church building offices are in charge of places of worship, the Regional Building offices in charge of state monument property. Monument conservation in the five new member states of Brandenburg, Mecklenburg-Western Pomerania, Saxony, Saxony-Anhalt, and Thuringia are undergoing a restructuring on this model.

Historic Preservation in the Federal Republic of Germany is represented abroad by bodies like the German National Committee for Monument Protection under the Federal Ministry of the Interior, the German National Committee of ICOMOS (International Council of Monuments and Sites) and the German Commission for UNESCO. Reports on preservation problems and results of work are given in the specialised reviews "Denkmalschutz-Informationen" (German National Committee, Bonn), "Deutsche Kunst und Denkmalpflege" (Munich/Berlin), "Die Alte Stadt" (Stuttgart), "Bautenschutz und Bausanierung" (Cologne), "Zeitschrift für Kunsttechnologie und Konservierung" (Worms), "Maltechnik-Restauro" (Munich), "Arbeitsblätter für Restauratoren" (the Roman-Germanic Central Museum of Mainz).

Ingrid Brock / Heinrich Magirius

The past as a warning to the present: the ruins of the belfry of the Kaiser-Wilhelm Memorial Church in Berlin, built in 1891–95 and destroyed in the Second World War, were incorporated into the new building designed by Egon Eiermann. Today not only the ruins but also the reinforced-concrete structure of the modern church, corroded by air pollution, is in need of extensive repair and consolidation measures.

The former Klosterkirche St. Michael (monastery church of St. Michael) in Hildesheim (Lower Saxony), built between 1007 and 1033; above: condition after the damage inflicted in the Second World War; below: reconstruction (1961) as a return to a scientifically established ideal form. In 1986, St. Michael's was included in the UNESCO World Heritage List together with Hildesheim Cathedral.

The History Museum on the Hohes Ufer in Hanover (architect Dieter Oesterlen, 1966): the staggered sections of the modern facade follow the old course of the street and correspond to the few historic half-timbered houses which could be saved after the Second World War.

During the Reichskristallnacht (Reich Crystal Night) of 9 November, 1938, nearly all of the synagogues in Germany were set on fire and destroyed; only in the countryside did some of them elude this fate, they were mostly worn out as sports halls, fire stations or barns. Today, monument conservators as well as public and private initiatives are trying hard to save them. In the photograph, the restored synagogue and adjoining Judenhäuser (jews' houses) in Kriegshaber near Augsburg (1992).

The "Angelic Greeting" in the hall choir of the Lorenzkirche (St. Lorenz Church) in Nuremberg, carved in 1517/18 by Veit Stoss. Up to nineteen restorers from Germany and abroad worked for one and a half years under the direction of the Bavarian Regional Office for Monument Conservation on the restoration of the limewood sculpture, which weighs 10.5 hundredweight and is suspended freely. The work was concluded in time for the Dürer Year of 1971.

The "Burgviertel" in the historic centre of Nuremberg, eighty percent of which was destroyed in the Second World War. In 1950, the Town Council had already laid down guidelines for its reconstruction, which prescribed the extensive preservation of the original street network, building heights, specific roof shapes and slopes, etc., thereby ensuring that the town regained its external physiognomy.

Regensburg in Bavaria: the old town, covering 177 hectares, the centre of which goes back to a Roman camp, was placed under a protection order on the basis of the Bavarian Law for Monument Preservation in December 1975. This conservation area includes 1050 individual monuments, predominantly from the medieval golden age of the town.

The docklands in the harbour are one of Hamburg's atmospheric districts. Some of these storehouses, in which coffee, spices, carpets, and other commodities have been handled since the end of the previous century, still retain their original function. A careful rehabilitation of this unique monument of industrial archaeology appears certain after its protection order.

Abandoned row of houses in Quedlinburg (Saxony-Anhalt): owing to the one-sided promotion of prefabrication in the building industry (types of prefabricated panelled building) and the suppression of self-employed crafts as well as any other private initiative in the former GDR, the decline of historic substance in the old towns was tremendously precipitated.

In the inner city area of Leipzig, 1991: as proof of historic monuments, however, the empty-standing trade buildings can only convey a fragmentary impression of what was the greatest 19th-century German historic centre up to 20 years ago.

The castles and gardens of Berlin-Potsdam, Summer residences of the Prussian kings and German emperors in the 18th and 19th centuries, form a unique "ensemble", which was included in the UNESCO World Heritage List in 1991 as the first all-German work. In the picture, the Schloss Sanssouci (designed by Georg W. von Knobelsdorff, 1745–47) with the restored vineyard terraces and the great fountains.

Saarbrücken, Residence: after year long discussions and an expert process, the middle section, which had been destroyed during the French Revolution, was not reconstructed according to the original plans by Friedrich Joachim Stengel (mid 18th century) but was erected by Gottfried Böhm in a contemporary architectural form.

Rapidly increasing erosion is threatening more and more of the existing historic monuments, especially masonry, stained-glass windows, and open-air sculptures. For several years, extensive programmes for research into possible causes and methods of conservation have been financed by the Federal Ministry of Research and Technology in Bonn and by the German Research Association (DFG).

The example shows a detail from the sculpture of the Crucifixion by Hans Backoffen (about 1500) in Bad Wimpfen, District of Heilbronn (Baden-Württemberg). The apparent damage consists mainly of the flaking-off of a thin surface layer, powdery decay, and flowering residue, and is probably due to an aggressive caustic solution and the influence of sulphates.

The Bauhaus building in Dessau, built by Walter Gropius in 1925/26.

Design

In the major industrial nations, classical modernism as the expression of the structuring of all spheres of life found its valid form in the years from 1920 onwards. In Germany a crucial focus of the new ideas was the "Bauhaus", founded in 1919 by Walter Gropius as a "College for Design", which dealt with every area of human requirements. This affected industrial mass production of everyday objects as well as architecture, concepts of contemporary fashion and living, and finally representation in graphic and photographic form, the design of the media.

These days, the "Bauhaus" school is often seen as the source of an exclusively techno-rational, "functionalist" design, but its members were by no means an undivided group with uniform ideas of proper form and proper content – on the contrary, they operated in a very lively experimental workshop, in which approaches to practically all the design concepts now current were developed. Direct confrontation with the trends of the fine arts also played its part: Wassily Kandinsky, Paul Klee, and László Moholy-Nagy were "Bauhaus" teachers.

In 1933, the "Bauhaus" also came to an end: freedom of thought did not correspond to the National Socialists' sole claim to design and programmatic self-portrayal. But in certain areas, National Socialism too considered efficiency and rationality desirable, and besides a style of design characterized by imperial pomp, prestige and impressiveness, there are designs for the office of "Beauty of Work", which in reality followed the methods of the officially condemned ideas of the classical modernists, thus also those of the "Bauhaus". Its most important leading figures emigrated in 1933, Walter Gropius, Herbert Bayer, and László Moholy-Nagy working at the "New Bauhaus" in Chicago. In Germany modernism had for the time being come to an end.

After 1945 in the Western part of Germany another "College for Design" in Ulm took up the "Bauhaus" tradition, which was still definitely modern. In 1955 the college was officially founded after a long period of preparation and moved into its own building, whose architect, the Swiss Max Bill, was also its first director. It was at that time that the English word "design" began to be accepted in German linguistic usage as well, at first only for technological industrial products and only later in the wide range of meaning common today. For a long time, modern design was almost identical with the Braun Company products, whose appearance was influenced by Ulm designers.

In 1968 "Ulm" too was at an end: whether because of the external resistance of a conservative environment, or rather because the institution had exhausted itself in too many internal debates, is still the subject of controversy. In any case, the sober, functional Ulm style did not exactly correspond to the popular trends of the young Republic with its explosion of multiplicity of form: kidney-shaped tables, jacaranda wood, brass and formica recalled a late version of art nouveau, while, on the other hand, imitative historical styles adapted from period furniture ("Gelsenkirchen Baroque") dominated the concept of a cosy home.

Accordingly, notions of the correct understanding of design then underwent very diverse developments, from a strictly functional design for innovative products of the capital-goods industry to dainty forms of self-portrayal in the personal sphere – all variants became possible and legitimate. Design is as manifold as people's ideas of what is right or important, and a reappraisal of the long-ignored design style of the 50s was eventually inevitable.

As a collaborator in a team, the designer naturally cannot rely only on subjective feelings. He must deal with the framework of technological and economic conditions; aerodynamics determine the shape of fast transport, and ergonomy is the basis for designing a place of work – the designer in industry must know about the normative conditions of his working field and understand the workings of the division of labour. Since design as a qualifying factor is constantly gaining in importance, he should also have a good knowledge of international markets: it is not uncommon for the design of American or Japanese products to have originated with German designers, who for their part may turn to the finest achievements of Italian designers – an international style is coming into being, in which national qualities set the particular emphases.

The designer has more freedom of play regarding products intended for the private sphere; here, with unique objects, he can risk experiments in design which are more usually allocated to the field of fine arts. But with increasing standardization and levelling of technical standards, the demand for unusual and eccentric design is also growing. Objects that previously stayed in the drawer as toys, now advertise the wealth of ideas and originality in design, which, however, cannot simply by reproduced at will, and, as reproductions of originality, are reduced to the point of absurdity.

Clothing, the object closest to the human being in every sense, demands every conceivable expression of individuality from fashion design: what appeals is allowed, and the ideas of what appeals are changing faster than ever. German fashion design, which traditionally had more of a reputation for modelling itself on Paris or Rome, developed an increasingly individual profile in international competition. Enterprises such as "Boss" or "Escada" have in a short time achieved a considerable reputation in the field of sophisticated ready-to-wear clothing. Between this field and the experiments of the *scene,* lies a wide area, in which, just as in product design, the designer stock markets have made themselves felt – stock markets where, besides the traditional presentations of new fashion, the rising generation has the opportunity to show its proposals for the possibilities of tomorrow.

The spreading of design trends would be unthinkable without the media and pictures: the photographic designers, usually in collaboration with graphic designers, have the job of depicting products, or mediating between manufacturers and clients, and of congenially interpreting and advertising the ideas and concepts of the product and fashion designers. They present their themes in a subjective, personally appealing way. To the graphic designer in particular, an inexhaustible repertoire is available for the realization of his ideas: from typography to naturalistic representation, from photography to collage and computer animation – such is the range of the technical possibilities for visual representation.

The design professions influence our everyday environment in many and various ways, and they give objects their sensorily perceptible form. Both in the positive and in the negative sense, it also follows that they bear a special, substantial responsibility. But they do this neither more nor less than anyone else who – in a highly differentiated industrial culture characterized by the division of labour – contributes his bit to shaping it – but the designers play an extremely interesting role in this.

In order to supply a sense of direction in the bewildering multitude of possibilities, the "Federation of Freelance Photographic Designers" publishes annuals, in which its members present themselves through typical examples of their work, while the annuals of the German "Art Directors Club" show the works of graphic and photographic designers, selected by a jury as outstanding achievements. Information about current trends in fashion design is provided by the fashion fairs in Munich, Düsseldorf and Berlin; and a selection of industrial design chosen by a jury is compiled in the catalogues for the annual special show "Good Industrial Design" of the Hanover Fair, as well as of the design centres in a number of Federal *Länder.*

If we turn our attention to the post-war history of design in the Eastern part of Germany, the first thing we must be aware of is the fact that, indeed, design as a universally disseminated culture of everyday use must necessarily awaken the interest of a totalitarian system – but that on the other hand the concrete working opportunities for the designer will be defined in the first place by the needs of industry. Thus the most marked differences between the political and social systems of the Federal Republic and the former GDR in design are mainly evident on the detour via the differing capacity of the popular industries. While peak achievements of industrial design had a real chance of realization in the free market economy of the Federal Republic of Germany, in the socialist planned economy of the GDR they remained stuck as a rule in the draft stage. Only too rarely did they go into production, so that they had no taste-forming influence on the public and could awaken no pleasure in good design.

The cultural heritage on which the self-image of an industrial society builds was the same after the war for the Federal Republic and the GDR; in some respects the people responsible for design in the GDR could more rightly have regarded themselves as the legitimate inheritors of the "Bauhaus" in Dessau – even if it took a remarkably long time before the inheritance was accepted.

At first, in any case, officialdom allowed the "Bauhaus" to crumble in both material and intellectual respects: the prejudice of the Party standpoint was for a long time an obstacle to the adoption of "bourgeois" "Bauhaus" ideas. But then everything happened with German thoroughness: the cultivation of this cultural heritage was also entrusted to the "Office for Industrial Design", whose leader, with ministerial rank, was supposed to develop awareness of design in the people and the "nationally-owned businesses", from a central position. This meant that design naturally had an official and socially much higher relative value than designers in the old Federal Republic could have dreamed of – yet at the same time the affair recalled much too vividly the intentions of the National Socialist "Office for Beauty of Work": design for the state-defined interests of human beings. This of course enables the excesses of a free market to be prevented – but at the price of a stage-governed peace and good order. The general public in the West was scarcely aware that, apart from the involuntary parody of the motor car's symbolism of freedom in the "Trabi", or the terribly fussy modernity of a "Wartburg", other things were also possible. But the potential is there: what the designers in the five new *Länder* can do can be demonstrated just as well as the achievements of their colleagues from the West.

Reinhold L. Hilgering/Olaf Hoffmann

Casual adaptation of the styles of classical elegance: from the "Escada" Collection 1988/89.

Experimental products of the fashion scene: punk outfit combined with knitwear, shown at the annual Munich "Avant-Garde" fair.

Children's fashion: what appeals is allowed, and photo-designer Sigi Bumm joins the cheerful game.

Continuous further development of form, retaining basic elements which symbolize the identity of the firm: comparison of the front section of Mercedes limousines vintage 1968, 1977, and 1987.

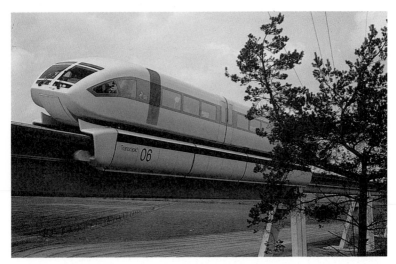

With the "Transrapid" express traffic system new techniques are being tested. The planning and coordination of this joint project by several firms confront the designer with special problems (design: Alexander Neumeister, Munich).

Design dream and production reality in the former GDR: above, a bodywork study by E. Scharnowski, K. Arndt, M. Rogge and J. Götze from the College of Design Burg Giebichenstein near Halle, from 1976; below, the motor car's everyday reality in the "Trabant", nicknamed "Trabi", for which GDR citizens accepted delivery periods of up to 14 years.

Long-term design and change of values: designed in 1936, this telephone was produced by Siemens & Halske almost unchanged up to 1960 before it was overtaken by progress. In the eighties it experienced a comeback as a collector's item, ultimately leading to its being officially made available again by the German Federal Post Office/Telecom, as a "nostalgia 'phone'".

Functional forms in the fifties: Phonosuper SK 4/SK 5 by Braun Co. Ltd., the famous "Snow-White's coffin", designed by Hans Gugelot and Dieter Rams.

Classical design in the style of the twenties and a reminder of the lost consumer world of the GDR: "Sprachlos" cigarillos. ▶

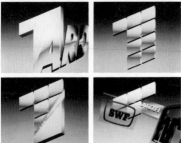

Achieved with the latest computer graphics: the new imprint of the ARD television channel and some stages of animation.

"Milan" was the name given by designer M. Böttcher from Halle to this "armchair with bearing surfaces", which enriched the functions of "sitting" and "reclining" with the imagination of flying.

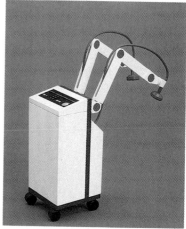

Short-wave impulse apparatus by B. Glier, C. Geyer and M. Marschhauser, Berlin: high ergonomic adaptation to patients calls for a universal design concept.

Studios and outdoor grounds of the Bavaria Studio Company, one of Europe's last big film factories in Munich-Geiselgasteig. Top left (can also be seen in the top left-hand corner of the aerial photograph), the scenery for the "Berlin Street" built for Ingmar Bergman's film *The Serpent's Egg* and also used in Rainer Werner Fassbinder's television film of Döblin's novel *Berlin Alexanderplatz*. Top right, the dragon Fuchur, built as a mobile model for Wolfgang Petersen's film of Michael Ende's *Never-Ending Story*.

Film and Television

Film

Early in 1976 the lead story in the magazine *Newsweek* was headed "The German Film Boom". The success of the German film abroad began in 1979, with Fassbinder's *The Marriage of Maria Brown* and continued with the Oscar awarded to Volker Schlöndorff's adaptation of Grass's *Tin Drum* and with the world-wide respect accorded to Wolfgang Petersen's *The Boat* and the work of Wim Wenders. It was the result of a lengthy development, starting with a manifesto: in 1962, during the West German Short Film Festival in Oberhausen, young directors announced their demand for a revival of the cinema of the Federal Republic. A difficult task: the gap torn by National Socialism in German film culture was too great; the qualitative deficit of national production in the fifties was among the late results. The "old" directors seemed to their future young colleagues to be representatives of the "corny cartel". Viewed artistically, the young German directors began as an orphaned generation.

Things were different in the films of the former GDR. The far-reaching international innovative movements which influenced film across the world in the sixties certainly passed by the GDR almost without trace, but production there had already undergone its decisive revival immediately after the war. Whereas the cinema of the then Western zones of occupation (the later Federal Republic of Germany) made a beginning with the manufacture of undemanding comedy, in the Soviet occupation zone of the time (the later GDR) they began with energetic attempts to make a critical re-appraisal of the most recent German past. The first of many subsequent anti-fascist films was Wolfgang Staudte's *The Murderers are Amongst Us.* The most important achievement of the DEFA, the state film production of the former GDR, consisted in the development and cultivation of an anti-fascist tradition which was maintained until reunification. Just about all the more important directors in the GDR made a contribution to this. Konrad Wolf, for instance, with *Ich war 19* and *Mama, ich lebe,* Frank Beyer with *Nackt unter Wölfen, Jakob der Lügner* and *Der Aufenthalt,* Gerhard Klein with *Der Fall Gleiwitz,* Slatan Dudow with *Stärker als die Nacht,* Kurt Maetzig with *Der Rat der Götter,* Günther Rücker and Günter Reisch with *Die Verlobte* and many others. Viewed artistically, these films are among the peak achievements of the former GDR cinema.

In the old Federal Republic as well, confrontations with the past had begun early, for instance with Helmut Käutner's *In jenen Tagen,* but the work seldom achieved an analytical dimension. Despite some successful entertainment films with critical motifs, such as those realized by Kurt Hoffmann *(Wir Wunderkinder),* Harald Braun *(Nachtwache),* Helmut Käutner *(Der Hauptmann von Köpenick),* West German production increasingly fell behind in the face of the attractions of Hollywood. Attempts by emigrants, such as Fritz Lang or Robert Siodmak, to work again in their old homeland met with little success.

The first efforts at renewal in the second half of the fifties came from those who were then outsiders. The Swiss Bernhard Wicki made the anti-war film *Die Brücke* in the Federal Republic. Two years earlier the Stuttgart neurologist Ottomar Domnick, working with author Hans Magnus Enzensberger, depicted the psychological isolation of modern urban man in *Jonas,* using avant-garde means. In the year of the Oberhausen Manifesto the Austrian Herbert Vesely provoked vigorous debates with his film version of Böll's *Das Brot der frühen Jahre.*

The decisive new beginning had its origins in 1966/67. The "new German film" became a concept – comparable with the French *nouvelle vague.* Supported by the "Committee for the Young German Film", many directors who had up to then gathered experience only with short films, were unexpectedly able to produce their first full-length films. These included Alexander Kluge, with *Abschied von gestern,* one of the first to realize the new film language promised in the Oberhausen Manifesto. In his confrontation with the present in the Federal Republic, taking as an example a young woman emigrant from the GDR who comes into conflict with Western society, Kluge created a montage of fictitious and documentary scenes and observed with curiosity, where other directors simply tried to substantiate their own theories. Closeness to the documentary was the characteristic feature of this first wave of film, which included Edgar Reitz's *Mahlzeiten,* Ulrich Schamoni's *Es,* Peter Schamoni's *Close Season for Foxes* and Haro Senft's *Der sanfte Lauf.* A special position among them was occupied by Volker Schlöndorff's film of Musil's *Young Törless,* a stylistically astonishingly complete first film, and Jean-Marie Straub's radically innovative *Not Reconciled,* an adaptation of Böll's novel *Billiards at Half-Past Nine.*

The box-office successes of the young directors soon began to fade like a fashion trend. The attempts to play critically with the set pieces of Hollywood action cinema, undertaken by Klaus Lemke with *48 Hours to Acapulco* and Rainer Werner Fassbinder with his first feature film *Liebe ist kälter als der Tod,* largely remained without consequences. The efforts to give new life to the very German cinematic genre of the "regional film" by means of political commitment and new positions, for instance with *Der plötzliche Reichtum der armen Leute von Kombach* by Volker Schlöndorff, or *Matthias Kneissl* by Reinhard Hauff, only temporarily touched the interest of a wider public. Things went little better for directors such as Christian Ziewer *(Liebe Mutter, mir geht es gut)* or Max Willutzki *(Der lange Jammer),* who were trying to revive in Berlin the tradition of the proletarian cinema interrupted by National Socialism.

After that hopeful beginning, the "new German film" soon experienced its first crisis, aggravated by the conflict between old and young among the producers and directors. The law on film subsidies – an economic law, because owing to the cultural authority of the *Länder* a cultural law at Federal level was not possible – produced some profitable serial productions, through which the work of the young film-makers was marginalized. The only certain way to success was the screening of literary works; this has as much to do with the affinity of German culture for the written word as with the significance of the scripts to film promotion: in the committees they are sometimes studied only word by word – but not picture by picture. Volker Schlöndorff's adaptation of Böll's *The Lost Honour of Katharina Blum,* his film version of the *Tin Drum* and also his latest work, *Homo Faber,* after the novel by Max Frisch, are among the positive examples of a trend which also produced many uninspired and academically conventional products, but did generally achieve a certain attention. Even the great box-office success of Wolfgang Petersen's *Never-ending Story* would have been scarcely conceivable without the popularity of the novel of the same name by Michael Ende – nor could the expensive production have been financed without that background.

The trend towards literature, though to different authors, is also observable in the cinema of the former GDR. The most popular authors were Arnold Zweig, Johannes R. Becher and Heinrich Mann. In contrast to the cinema of the Federal Republic, the DEFA also produced some outstanding scriptwriters, above all Wolfgang Kohlhaase.

In the Federal Republic, on the other hand, a trend produced by the concept of a purely authorial cinema gained ground, when the directors also began to create their own scenarios. This also fitted in with the resolution of the film-makers to go their own way undeterred, to insist on an unmistakable signature and only ever to deal with themes which moved them personally. As an autodidact, Werner Herzog began with short films, which already reveal his subsequent almost obsessive insistence on his own particular cosmos of subjects and motifs. After artistically remarkable "smaller" works such as *Signs of Life* and *Land of Silence and Darkness,* Herzog also achieved international recognition with *Jeder für sich und Gott gegen alle,* which made it easier for him to finance bigger projects such as *Fitzcarraldo, Wo die grünen Ameisen träumen, Cobra Verde* and *Schrei aus Stein.* The famous film historian Lotte Eisner has called him "the new Murnau"; Friedrich Wilhelm Murnau (1888–1931) was probably the most important of all German cineastes.

No less single-minded was the development by Rainer Werner Fassbinder, who died in 1982 at the age of 37, of his own filmic cosmos, and he was always re-telling German history, up to the present day – except that he kept his distance from official history. Fassbinder's work is a great private chronicle of Germany and the Federal Republic, a chronicle of personal sufferings and private notions of happiness, which not infrequently ran in counterpoint to the successful economic development of the country. Thus *The Marriage of Maria Braun* tells of the price, too high in human terms, of prosperity during the reconstruction. *Lola,* based on Heinrich Mann's novel *Professor Unrat,* looks behind the attractive facades of the economic miracle with ironic humour. Fassbinder's sensitivity in the description of psychological injuries reached its culmination in the very private film *In einem Jahr mit 13 Monden* and in the Döblin-based film *Berlin Alexanderplatz* – really the director's chief work and masterpiece.

It is persistence that characterizes the great artists and enables their life's work to circle round a central theme. Thus Alexander Kluge's works always confront the question as to when the catastrophe of National Socialism really began and at what point it might still have been avoided. *The Patriot,* a film whose title figure literally begins to dig into German history, is a typical example of the question he is asking. While Kluge approaches this question intellectually, Hans Jürgen Syberberg surrounds it with narrative collages fascinated by myth: they range from *Karl May* via the Bavarian King *Ludwig II* and *Hitler – Ein Film aus Deutschland,* to the operatic film based on Richard Wagner's *Parsifal.*

Only a few of the many graduates of the Munich College of Television and Film and of the Film and Television Academy in Berlin have really succeeded up to now, including Wolfgang Petersen with his light entertainment films *Das Boot* and *Never-ending Story* and above all Wim Wenders, who in contrast to Petersen persists in his unmistakably personal style and equally unmistakable subject matter, constantly exploring the possibilities and impossibilities of human relations, moving from *Alice in den Städten,* via *Im Lauf der Zeit* and *Paris, Texas* to his masterpiece *Himmel über Berlin* and the very controversial, much debated *Bis ans Ende der Welt.* Wenders' time in Hollywood, when he was producing *Hammett* for Coppola, developed into a passion, which he reports in the form of a parable, but frankly, in *Der Stand der Dinge.*

The wealth of the German film is also and especially influenced by outsiders – for instance by the work of Werner Schroeter, who began with experimental attempts such as *Eika Katappa* and then reached a wider public with

Palermo oder Wolfsburg and more recently with *Malina;* or the provocative work of film-makers Rosa von Praunheim and Vlado Kristl, or by the cinematographic experiments of Werner Nekes, or by the film essays of Harun Farocki and Hellmuth Costard. And also by a film-maker such as Herbert Achternbusch, whose work is indivisibly linked with his Bavarian home – even when he was making the documentary film *Blaue Blumen* in China. Achternbusch, whose comedy follows on the complex humour of a Karl Valentin, has since the seventies been among the most imaginative of German film-makers – and the most uncomfortable, which has brought him no helpful friendships either in politics or in television. His film *Das Gespenst* caused some scandal, although he had previously received a Federal film prize for *Das letzte Loch.* He is the *poète maudit* of German film-makers, who records losses and secret destruction and keeps his spirit of contradiction alert with Bavarian stubbornness. In perhaps his most beautiful film, *Wanderkrebs,* he slips with self-directed irony into the costume of a court-jester guiding his sovereign on a sight-seeing tour through the shattered countryside of his country.

In the second half of the eighties the forms of American mainstream cinema further extended their predominant position in the German cinema as well. The situation of the outsider became still more difficult. So it was that many directors, including names as famous as Wenders, Schlöndorff, Schroeter, Herzog and Syberberg slipped away to productions in opera houses and state theatres.

Achternbusch wrote and produced stage plays and quite often realized his films only in Super 8 format. Kluge retired to a cultural magazine on private television.

This kind of outsider never existed in the GDR cinema, but despite the state control of the means of production, films were made which were prohibited or hindered by censorship. From today's standpoint it is clear that it was precisely the more courageous works with more exciting and aesthetic content that were suppressed – even when they came from well-known directors. It was not revealed until the late repeat performance of Frank Beyer's *Spur der Steine* what potential this director had available. Egon Günther's most intense work, *Die Schlüssel,* Konrad Wolf's *Sonnensucher,* Gerhard Klein's *Berlin um die Ecke,* Kurt Maetzig's *Das Kaninchen bin ich* and Jürgen Böttcher's *Jahrgang 45* were also among the suppressed films, which indicates what marvellous heights the cinema of the GDR might have achieved without the intervention of narrow-minded functionaries. One also gets an impression of this from the great documentary film-makers of the former GDR, Jürgen Böttcher and Volker Koepp, and more recently the film-maker Helke Misselwitz. Despite all the obstacles, brave, controversial work did appear successfully in the cinema: for instance Konrad Wolf's intelligent plea for the right to individualism with the programmatic title *Solo Sunny,* or Günter Reisch's cunning comedy in praise of private initiative on the margins of legality *Anton, der Zauberer.* In the former GDR the feature film (in contrast to the documentary) was the domain of men only. In the Federal Republic a few women at least were able to succeed as film-makers: Margarethe von Trotta with *Das zweite Erwachen der Christa Klages, Die bleierne Zeit* and *Rosa Luxemburg;* Doris Dörrie with her comedy *Männer* and Jeannine Meerapfel with *Malou,* while the two most aesthetically exciting German "women's films" had only a minor success: *Bildnis einer Trinkerin* by Ulrike Ottinger and *Der Schlaf der Vernunft* by Ula Stöckl.

The most recent generation is having an even more difficult time and retreating from the economic pressure in the cinema, preferably to television. Nevertheless some very promising talents have appeared in the last few years, although they have not been able to work nearly as continuously as the protagonists of the "new German film" in the late sixties. Among the successful debuts are *Schwarz und ohne Zucker* by Lutz Konermann, *Zischke* by Martin Theo Krieger, *Dorado One Way* by Reinhard Münster, *Drachenfutter* by Jan Schütte, *Kanakerbraut* and *Sierra Leone* by Uwe Schrader. Dominik Graf seems at present to be the only representative of a new generation who is not forced to delay for several years between individual films while searching for finance for a new project, and has been able to produce new work regularly even in the last few years, with *Die Katze,* mit *Tiger, Löwe, Panther* and *Der Spieler.* Michael Klier's much respected first film *Überall ist es besser, wo wir nicht sind* and its successor *Ostkreuz* did reach the cinema, but were actually produced as "small television plays". Talent alone is no longer enough; the rising generation needs an energetic capacity to win through, if it is to make its way artistically.

The positive development experienced by the West German cinema in the seventies would have been inconceivable without extensive measures of promotion. The "German film miracle" is also the result of subsidies, debates on film policy and other supportive measures, including not least the "general agreement" between the film industry and television, first concluded in 1974; in this agreement the television stations of the Federal Republic of Germany undertake to make considerable resources available for co-productions with film producers and to allow the film thus co-produced a prior showing period in the cinema of, as a rule, two years. The most noted and debated promotion measure for the German film consists in the "Law on Film Subsidies". The aim of this law is "to augment the quality of the German film on a broad basis and to improve the structure of the film industry" with the help of financial assistance bound by specific conditions. The measure to which most attention is paid by the public is undoubtedly the

"German Film Award", intended "to distinguish and encourage outstanding achievements". The awards (Golden Bowl, Film Ribbon) for the best film and other outstanding films (both long and short) in one year, as well as for individual artistic achievement (direction, camera, etc.) for the most part involve cash prizes. Through the decree of the Federal Minister of the Interior in 1964 the "Committee for the New German Film" was also created. The Committee concentrates, according to its constitution, on the promotion of projects by film novices (and the second works of beginners). Since the first wave of the new German film in the sixties the Committee has played a part which can scarcely be over-estimated in the artistic development of modern German cinema. In the eighties most of the Federal *Länder* have also taken certain measures to promote the film. Those with considerable financial means are above all the film promotion boards in Bavaria and Berlin, but Hamburg, North Rhine-Westphalia and Hesse also energetically promote films in a way which sometimes goes beyond production and also applies to distribution and showing.

Although the modalities of the German film promotion system are controversially debated, production, distribution and film theatres are still dependent on subsidies, also faced with the overwhelming presence of the Hollywood film, which in 1990 took a market share of 83.8% in the Federal Republic, whereas the home production share sank to 9.7%. For 1991 the Film Promotion Institute announced an increase in turnover of some ten per cent for the 3,200 cinemas of the old Federal *Länder;* so far no figures are available as to the share of American and German production in the 108 million or so tickets sold. There is at present no reliable information as to the number of active film theatres in the five new Federal *Länder* since reunification; there is no sign of a cinema boom. Whereas in 1988 the cinemas of the former GDR could still record 87 million visitors, the estimate for the five new Federal *Länder* in 1991 is an audience figure of only some 12 million.

Hans Günther Pflaum

Scene-photograph from the film *Knife in the Head* by Reinhard Hauff showing Hans-Christian Blech (left) and Bruno Ganz.

Rainer Werner Fassbinder (1946–82) was one of the most productive directors and authors in film history. As examples of the 41 films and television series he produced in only 13 years, our pictures show: *The Marriage of Maria Braun* (1978) with Hanna Schygulla and George Bird (left): *The Bitter Tears of Petra von Kant* (1972) with Margit Carstensen and Hanna Schygulla (bottom left): *Dealer of the Four Seasons* (1971) with Kurt Raab (in the centre) (illustration below).

The films by Herbert Achternbusch (b. 1938) combine the Bavarian mentality with a surreal penetration of social conditions. The picture shows author, director, and actor Achternbusch (right) with Franz Baumgartner in *Wanderkrebs* (1984).

Distinguished at the Cannes Film Festival and with an American "Oscar" for the best foreign production, Volker Schlöndorff's film of Günter Grass's novel *The Tin Drum* became one of the most successful German post-war films. From the left: author Grass, principal actor David Bennent, director Schlöndorff during shooting.

The first German post-war film was made in 1946 by the DEFA, later the film company monopoly in the GDR. In *Die Mörder sind unter uns* director Wolfgang Staudte attempted a first reappraisal of the crimes of National Socialism and the guilt which the Germans had incurred in the Second World War. Pictured above, Hildegard Knef and Ernst Wilhelm Borchert.

Wild West in East Germany: in the DEFA production *Spur der Steine* by Frank Beyer (1966) Manfred Krug played a self-assured team leader unwilling to accept the inefficiency of real socialism. The film was withdrawn from circulation in the GDR soon after its première and did not return to the cinema until the changeover.

Scene from the film *Woyzeck* by Werner Herzog after Georg Büchner's drama: Klaus Kinski as Woyzeck, Wolfgang Reichmann as the captain, Willy Semmelrogge as the doctor.

Volker Schlöndorff (b. 1939) with actresses Franziska Walser and Angelika Winkler (right) during the shooting of his contribution to the episodic film *Germany in Autumn* (1978).

Wim Wenders (b. 1945, ill. above right) is one of the internationally respected German film-makers. The picture below shows Bruno Ganz and Otto Sander in the roles of the guardian angels Damiel and Cassiel in his film *Wings of Desire*, which was awarded the prize for best direction in Cannes in 1988.

In her film *Bildnis einer Trinkerin,* premièred at the 13th International Hof Film Days in 1979, Ulrike Ottinger (book, camera and production) mapped out a "geography of Berlin for female drinkers". The photograph shows Raul Gimenes and Tabea Blumenschein.

Scene from *Der Schlaf der Vernunft* (1984) by Ula Stöckl, with Christoph Lindert and Ida di Benedetto.

Above: Werner Herzog (b. 1942) during the shooting of his film *Heart of Glass* (1976) with actor Wilhelm Friedrich.

Right: Klaus Kinski and Isabelle Adjani in Werner Herzog's remake of Murnau's classic *Nosferatu*.

Below: worker Bruno S. (right) played Stroszek in the film ballad of the same name by Werner Herzog. Centre. Clemens Scheitz: left. Clayton Szlapinski.

Tatort is the title of a series of crime films by ARD to which each associated regional network contributes its own inspector. In 1991 Günter Lamprecht was able to play the first inspector to pursue his enquiries after the collapse of the GDR in both West and East Berlin.

Television

It is 17.55 on Thursday, 9 November 1989. In its second programme, the "Television of the GDR" is transmitting live one of the last press conferences of the old SED. After some information on various subjects, the speaker pulls out a sheet of paper as if in passing, and reads the news of the decision to open the Wall and the Western borders of the GDR – an announcement carrying a restriction notice for 4.0 a.m. on Friday. It is thus that television brings the inconceivable news to the world – a casual announcement makes history. At once tens of thousands pour through the Brandenburg Gate to test the West. Television, from East and West, is there live, showing the internal and external movement of people. Every day of the weeks and months that follow is full of historic (television) events. Not just a medium but a factor of social developments of historic dimensions – that was television in that time of change, that turning-point.

Was it in fact the catalyst of revolution in East Germany, did it contribute to the escalation or, through the presence of electronic cameras, did it not rather prevent the outbreak of violence? Did it conjure up the first media revolution in history? The effects of television are long-term. In 1974 the associations of the KSZE laid the foundations for the working conditions of correspondents in the other German state, for more extensive information. The trans-border West German television programmes were more than ever in opposition to GDR internal and external propaganda after the Helsinki Conference, and this discrepancy undoubtedly contributed to the weakening of the state ideology. As it emerged after the "change", the mass of people in the GDR was aware through television of the sugar icing side of West Germany in particular. The cause lay in the selective awareness of the people, influenced by their comprehensive isolation: they wanted to see only the positive. The bright images of television advertising lingered more than the weaknesses of rigorously investigative articles in the political television magazine programmes. While the two big West German television programmes, ARD and ZDF, could be received throughout the GDR, apart from the Dresden area, the "valley of the clueless", and were watched with intense interest, East German state television reached only an insignificant part of West Germany. The attractive feature films on offer competed with the West German programmes wherever the former could be received, but scarcely any attention was paid in the West to the sterile propagandist news broadcasts and political programmes. Thus despite the information from correspondents in the media, the GDR was a practically unknown country to the great majority of West Germans, and conversely the East Germans thought they could see West Germany through the screen as the promised land. Result: Go West.

Flashback, more than a hundred years earlier: on Christmas Eve 1883 the student Paul Nipkow discovered the principle of image breakdown which some 50 years later was to enable television pictures to be transmitted over quite long distances – mechanically at first, with the help of the rotating "Nipkow disc", then electronically. The pioneering discovery in electronic television was made by the Nobel prizewinner Karl Ferdinand Braun in 1897: the "Braun tube". In 1906 this cathode ray tube was developed into an image receiver by his pupils Gustav Glage and Max Dieckmann. In 1930 Manfred von Ardenne succeeded in constructing a camera with an electronic image-receiving tube, with which he realized the first fully electronic television transmission. From March 1935 onwards the Reichspost broadcast a regular television programme and a year later the National Socialists made use of the new medium to transmit the events of the Olympic Games in 28 "television studios", small cinemas, for eight hours a day. Until the autumn of 1944 the television was used via cable networks, especially in Berlin, to raise the morale of wounded soldiers and those on home leave.

The revival of television in ruined Germany took longer than in the USA, the Soviet Union, England and France, where programmes were resumed immediately after the end of the war. Not until 1950 could experimental television broadcasts be begun in both the Federal Republic of Germany and the German Democratic Republic. On the first Christmas Day of 1952 the North West German broadcasting company (NWDR) began regular programme transmissions via transmitters in Hamburg and Hanover. From the autumn of 1954 the West German *Land* radio organizations, which had joined together in the "Association of West German Broadcasting Corporations under Public Law" (ARD), broadcast a joint programme. Television in the GDR started on 21 December 1952, from the new studio in Berlin Adlershof, a regular, experimental official programme, which on 3 January 1956 was expanded into a full television programme as "German Television Broadcasting" (DFF).

The two television systems developed in opposite directions: into a Federal, non-state television under public law in the Federal Republic and into a strictly centralized, state television in the GDR. The television systems in the two states on German soil took on diametrically opposite tasks. The "DFF" became the most important medium popularizing the policies of the SED and the government and intended to educate the citizens in socialist thought and action. Accordingly the programmes were filled with agitprop from the beginning. The "German television" of the ARD, on the other hand, was deliberately planned outside government influence, much to the annoyance of the governments of Konrad Adenauer between 1949 and 1963: a difficult learning process for directors and journalists, business managers and theatre managers on the one hand and politicians in the *Länder* and the

Federation on the other hand. The old, new medium of television played the role, especially from the sixties onwards, of a "third force" in the state. Both in East and West German television the news broadcasts "Tagesschau" (West) and "Aktuelle Kamera" (East) headed the programmes. But characteristic of the most extreme, typical statement of the new medium, was the television play, the valid expression of the first two decades of West German television. It created a revolution, leading from the performance of classical material and versions of Anglo-American comedies in the first decade, right through to the socio-critical, semi-documentary TV play of contemporary history in the sixties and seventies. Similar to a stage performance, the television play in the early years of television was at first produced and transmitted live in the studio. It was only the introduction of the video tape recording after 1958 that created the conditions for the development of a television-specific dramaturgy and aesthetic. At the same time it also set in motion a thorough-going alteration of the journalistic production conditions of topical and documentary programmes right up to the "electronic reporting" in use today, which largely replaced the film from 1978 onwards. This kind of extensive technical innovation, including colour television from 1967 onwards, was available to West German television only on the basis of dual financing: viewers' fees on the one hand and, from 1955 onwards, receipts from television advertising on the other hand. Viewing figures increasing by leaps and bounds thus had their dual effect on the amazing rise of television, from a medium for the few who in the fifties used to gather round the goggle-boxes in the pubs, to become the mass medium of today, with at least one television in every household. In 1957 the viewing figures in the West and in 1960 in the East passed the magic figure of one million reported sets – only then was it anchored in the public consciousness as a new medium. In 1960 an "advertising television" was finally introduced into the GDR as well – not for the financing of new, additional projects, but as a propaganda demonstration of industrial and political successes.

In the same year, 1960, newspaper and journal publishers, industry and advertising in the Federal Republic of Germany, supported by Federal guarantees, founded the first commercial television programme company, the "Free Television GmbH". Through the foundation of a similarly privately run umbrella company, which was nevertheless owned by the Federation, the "Germany Television GmbH", Federal Chancellor Konrad Adenauer provoked the first television judgement under Federal constitutional law, which stopped the "Adenauer Television". This failed attempt resulted in the foundation of the "Second German Television Channel" (ZDF), which on 1 April 1963 started its broadcasts, partly with programmes and people working on "Free television", and of five regional Third Television programmes of the Federal *Länder* between 1964 and 1969: "Study Programme" by the Bavarian Broadcasting, Munich, "Hesse III" from Frankfurt, "North III" from Hamburg, Berlin and Bremen, "WDF – West German Television" from Cologne and "S 3" from Stuttgart, Baden-Baden and Saarbrücken. While until the end of the sixties the ZDF developed as a full programme in competition with the ARD joint programme, the Third channels had the initial task for more than a decade of broadcasting cultural, educational and regional programmes. From the end of the seventies they too were expanded into full-scale programmes at the expense of their cultural and educational character, and schools television was reduced bit by bit. Only the "Telecollege", begun in Bavaria in 1967, a media-combined programme for night school, survived all the programme reforms, enabling tens of thousands to prepare themselves for technical or specialist college entry. With the similar goal of transmitting culture and education (although on a GDR socialist basis), a second television programme began in the GDR on 3 October 1969, but this too gradually sacrificed its educational character. For in the Federal Republic as well as in the GDR – though treated as confidential there until the days of the "Change" – viewing figures and sometimes also qualitative judgements of the programmes were ascertained, and it turned out that the figures for educational programmes were dropping towards zero in the course of the seventies: viewing figures began to govern programmes.

This tendency was reinforced after 1984, when commercial television was admitted into the Federal Republic – at first in the form of regional experimental projects, which passed imperceptibly into the general normality of a "dual" television system. The advertising revenues which financed the private transmitters are directly related to the viewing figures and thus necessarily exercise pressure on the programming: mass attraction threatens to become more important than criteria relating to content. Up to thirty regional, national and international television programmes are today fed into West German cable networks and/or received via satellites or terrestrially via ordinary house antennae. Four stations governed by public law (ARD, ZDF, Eins Plus, 3sat) and four commercial television programmes (RTL plus, SAT 1, Pro 7 and Tele 5) are broadcast nationally. In addition to these there are the Franco-German cultural channel "Arte", the news channel and the subscription channel "Premiere". Finally a number of international television programmes, including some from France, England and Turkey, can be received via satellite and over the cable networks. Since 1990/91 RTL plus and SAT 1 have been showing a profit. However, although the commercials broadcast for 24 hours a day and the public stations are following the trend to all-day programmes, the use of television has largely been concentrated in the peak viewing hours of 7–11 p.m. Roughly two-thirds of the whole programme of the two big national commercial television companies,

RTL plus and SAT 1, consist of feature films, series and game shows, while the share taken by information and education ranges between 10 and 14%. The big public companies, ARD and ZDF, broadcast about 30–50% information and educational programmes, with feature films, series and shows taking up some 40% of the whole programme. During the political changes in Eastern Europe in 1989, from the beginning of the German reunification process and in the Gulf War of 1991, the non-commercial programmes were able to exploit their strength in topical information, rapid live input and their far-ranging networks of correspondents and thus – perhaps only for a short time? – halt the trend towards fiction.

At the same time, however, they are now the biggest commissioners of feature and documentary film production in Germany. In the film-television agreement of 1974 (since renewed several times) ARD and ZDF guarantee co-productions with the film industry which are first shown in the cinema and then on television after a specific waiting period. The commercial programmes broadcast almost exclusively bought-in films and series – mainly produced abroad. Their share in their own production of fiction is still quite insignificant, but will undoubtedly increase when they have an improved financial basis. Some 100 medium-sized and large television programme suppliers contributed in 1991 to the non-fiction share in commercial and also in public television programmes.

The chief problem in new German television at present is to bring into line the media systems in East and West, which have been incompatible for 40 years. Between the day of reunification on 3 October 1990, and 31 December 1991, the East German "DFF-*Länder* chain" broadcast a central programme with small regional programme windows. The central, over-staffed institutions of television and radio, up to then strictly separate in their organization, were dissolved and thousands of technicians, programmers and administrators were released on to the media market; radio and television in the new Federal *Länder* were linked in each case under a single aegis and the dual system of public and private television programmes introduced. At the beginning of 1992 the newly-founded public national broadcasting organizations which had first been distanced from the state in 1932, took over independent programming in East Germany. In Saxony, Saxony-Anhalt, Thuringia, Brandenburg and Mecklenburg-Western Pomerania, their own *Land* broadcasting laws and laws on private broadcasting were passed in the spring and summer of 1991. On the basis of these laws, Saxony, Saxony-Anhalt and Thuringia established "Central German Broadcasting" (MDR) on 30 May 1991 by inter-state contract with headquarters in Leipzig and *Land* broadcasting stations in Halle, Dresden, Magdeburg and Erfurt. The new, old name represents the tradition of broadcasting in the media town of Leipzig, where in 1924 the MIRAG ("Central German Broadcasting

AG") was founded, as one of the oldest German broadcasting companies. This historical link was decided on, even though nowadays the MDR is no longer in central Germany but in the south-east of united Germany. Whereas the MDR, as a three *Länder* organization, is now among the large members of the ARD combine, the Federal *Land* of Brandenburg ventured to go it alone with the foundation of "East German Broadcasting Brandenburg" (ODR), creating another small institution which was dependent from the start on the financial and programming aid of the larger ARD members. The *Land* of Mecklenburg-Western Pomerania went a different way, associating itself through an inter-state contract with North German Broadcasting, so that as a four-*Länder* institute it has still greater importance in the ARD "concert". Besides their shares in the first programme, the ARD joint programme, ODR and MDR each put together their own Third Television programmes, as do the other ARD institutions. They and the NDR station in Rostock help to record the "state" of the people in East Germany and to reshape it, more or less cautiously. The Second German Television, as a central institution, attempts to achieve this with a widely branching network of *Land* studios and correspondents. In 1992 the expansion and allocation of frequencies to commercial television suppliers is beginning in all five East German Federal *Länder*.

Perceptive as no other medium, television broadcast to the whole world the attempts to leave or break out of the former GDR and ultimately the tears of joy when the Wall fell. Its initial task in this decade is to help to overcome the Wall in the hearts and minds of the people in the coalescent Germany. At the same time, as a crossfrontier medium, it influences European unification. How all these great demands on programmes, makers and organizations can be reconciled with the simultaneous cost explosion on programmes and the constantly re-divided advertising cake – that is the big question mark over the last television decade of this millennium.

Rüdiger Steinmetz

One of the greatest artistic successes in the history of German television was the eleven-part family chronicle *Heimat* (1986), in which Edgar Reitz (direction) and Peter Steinbach (script collaboration) told the history of Germany in the twentieth century, reflected in the microcosm of a Hunsrück village. In the photograph, from left to right, actors Eva Maria Schneider, Karin Rasenack, Sabine Wagner, Anke Jendrychowski, Hans Jürgen Schatz, and Johannes Lobewein.

Robert Lembke, who died in January of 1989, wrote television history with his "cheerful job-guessing" game *Was bin ich?,* which for 33 years enjoyed the audience's favour.

The audience determines the programme of the *ARD Wunschkonzert* with Max Schautzer and Dagmar Berghoff.

The detective series *Derrick,* named after the investigating television inspector Stefan Derrick, is one of the major foreign-licenced successes of ZDF and is being broadcast worldwide, even in Japan. The picture shows the hero, played by Horst Tappert (left), with his assistant Harry Klein (played by Fritz Wepper).

The cabaret shows of the "Münchner Lach- und Schiessgesellschaft" (the picture shows Jochen Busse, Renate Küster, Henning Venske, and Rainer Basedow) are regularly broadcast by television, as are those of the Düsseldorf "Kommödchen". Dieter Hildebrandt presents with a variety of guests his monthly programme *Scheibenwischer* on the channel Sender Freies Berlin especially for television.

Under the slogan *Essen wie Gott in Deutschland,* award-winning chefs reveal their cooking secrets. In the photograph: Munich's star chefs Maureen and Otto Koch.

Presenter Kurt Zimmermann in a special broadcast by the cultural magazine *Titel Thesen Temperamente* on the Frankfurt Book Fair.

Wetten dass …? (ZDF) has become one of the most popular family shows on Saturday evenings, thanks in great part to the popularity of the presenters Frank Elstner and (pictured) Thomas Gottschalk.

Television camera before the Berlin Wall by the Brandenburg Gate on 10 November 1989: a symbolic image of the role of the electronic media in the GDR's gentle revolution that opened the way to the reunification of Germany.

On the eve of reunification, 2 October 1990, historian Michael Stürmer, writer Günter ▶ Grass and politicians Egon Bahr and Wolfgang Schäuble in the special broadcast "What now, Germany?", which was transmitted from the Berlin Reichstag building. Far left and right, moderators Klaus-Peter Siegloch and Klaus Bresser.

Dresden in upheaval: Dresden artists demonstrating for freedom of art and opinion in front of the Semper Opera House on 19 November 1989. At the microphone TV showmaster and opera singer Gunther Emmerlich.

Pro und Contra, presented by Ernst Elitz, puts topical themes of discussion to the vote of the studio audience after consulting a panel of experts.

The ZDF series *Das Verkehrsgericht* demonstrates traffic law in cases taken from real life.

Veto (ARD), presented by Heinz Burghart, sees itself as a mouthpiece of the citizen.

The ARD political magazines are broadcast regularly at 9 p.m. on Tuesday. As an example, the photo shows the editorial team of *Monitor* with (from l. to r.) Albrecht Reinhardt, Jürgen Thebrath, Wolfgang Landgraeber, Dr. Klaus Bednarz, Irmgard Grosskopf, and Volker Happe.

The nightmare of a "Stasi" continuing in post, having survived the GDR, was depicted in one of the last DFF television plays, broadcast on 3 October 1991 by the ARD on the first anniversary of reunification: *Häschen hüpf* by Ulrich Plenzdorf with Thomas Neumann (photo).

"ZDF special" on the People's Chamber elections in the GDR on 18 March 1990: Michael Schmitz in conversation with election winner Lothar de Maizière and loser Ibrahim Böhme. Both politicians were later charged with collaboration with the GDR State Security Service ("Stasi"), and withdrew.

Culture, politics, and science: representing many other "TV personalities" we show here Hans-Jürgen Rosenbauer, Dieter Kronzucker, and Heinz Haber.

Native songs, folk music, and choirs have a loyal audience. Shown here is the Tölz Boys' Choir at a request concert.

"The most important triviality in the world" is covered by ZDF's *Aktuelles Sportstudio* (above), ARD's *Sportschau,* and many special broadcasts on outstanding individual events by both channels.

ARD (Association of West German Broadcasting Corporations Under Public Law) and ZDF (Second German Television) cover the entire area of the Federal Republic of Germany with their broadcasts. ARD comprises the regional broadcasting companies: Bavarian Broadcasting (BR), Hessian Broadcasting (HR), North German Broadcasting (NDR), Radio Bremen (RB), Saarland Broadcasting (SR), West-Berlin Broadcasting (SFB), South German Broadcasting (SDR), Southwestern Broadcasting (SWF), and West German Broadcasting (WDR), and in the new Federal *Länder* Central German Broadcasting (MDR) and East German Broadcasting Brandenburg (ORB). Limited to the regions, these broadcasting companies also run a "Third Programme", originally conceived as a programme for education and minorities, which has in the meantime been largely expanded into a full programme.

In addition, private channels have been established for some years now, such as Sat 1, RTL plus, Pro 7, Tele 5 and 3 Sat (the latter a merger of ZDF and Swiss and Austrian television), which can be received in part via satellite, in part via cable.

In every part of the Federal Republic of Germany, a large variety of traditional festivities keeps the past alive. Above, the Dinkelsbühl "Kinderzeche", recalling the saving of the town from the Swedes in the Thirty Years War. Below, the Fishermen's Competition, which takes place every four years on the Danube in Ulm.

Customs and Festivals

Customs are a greeting from the good old days – says popular opinion, although the old days were sometimes not so good at all. Many customs which still seem to us romantic and worth preserving today, and of which we are fond, go back to quite prosaic events. Nor should we forget that the two now reunited parts of Germany went their very different ways in this respect in the last 45 years. For in the former GDR the celebration of customs was suppressed until the mid-seventies. Later there was some re-thinking in the SED and mass organizations.

Organized in folklore centres, the "Preservation of the cultural heritage under the aegis of socialism" was now intended to encourage the citizens' love of country. So up and down the land ancient festivals were revived, converted into a mixture of propaganda event and exhibition, with a colourful sprinkling of regional folklore.

Customs and festivals frequently go together, because at the great ecclesiastical, historical, country, or heathen festivals customs unfold all their splendour, and on the other hand the inherited customs transform the local festivities, traditional processions, and the fairs featuring shooting matches into something special. And it is remarkable that in our highly technological, computer-oriented age, more and more young people discover and foster their love of tradition.

Beside the folk music fairs and costume processions to be found everywhere between the North Sea and the Baltic, the Black Forest, the Harz Mountains and the Alps, this applies above all to the country festivals throughout the seasons. With fireworks and whip-cracking, with gun salutes and rowdy romping of terrifyingly disguised figures the evil spirits are sent packing and the New Year is protected from them. And in addition, people try to secure themselves a little happiness and prosperity for the coming twelve months. They give each other good-luck symbols such as clover-leaves, horseshoes, or little chimney sweeps made of every conceivable material, they keep a scale from the carp eaten on New Year's Eve in their purses or try to read the fate that awaits them by dropping molten lead into cold water and interpreting the resulting shapes.

On 6 January the pre-Lent period begins, in which the people not only chase away the demons of winter but also celebrate the already lengthening days. In Bavaria this crazy period is known as *Fasching,* in the Rhineland-Palatinate as *Fastnacht* and in North Rhine-Westphalia and New Brandenburg as *Karneval.* As well as the big, perfectly organized Rose Monday (day before Shrove Tuesday) processions in the *Fasching* strongholds on the Rhine and Main, more customary forms of the Festival were held in many places. Thus in parts of Baden-Württemberg they celebrate the masquerade of the Swabian-Alemannic *Fastnacht;* at the Voigtland *"Fosnet"* everything is centred on the legendary figure of the "Pumphut", a creature endowed with magic powers of the fairy tale world there, which does good to good people and punishes the wicked. At the Munich Food Market the market women, and everyone who wants to be there on that day, dance on Shrove Tuesday. In Buchholz in Mark Brandenburg the children dress up as witches and play tricks on the grown-ups before flying to the Bocksberg. At the miners' *Fastnacht* in Goslar the "masked men" tease the girls with their pigs' bladders filled with peas, and in the Lausitz the wild *Zamperbrüder* go to *"Zapust"* on their begging round from house to house and then divide their spoils at the evening feast. And then, after the carnival hurly-burly, Lent begins in all the hotels, restaurants and public houses with a usually rather opulent meal of fish.

On Laetare Sunday, the fourth Sunday after Ash Wednesday, a very special type of festival takes place in Eisenach. In the "Summer Victory", "Frau Sunna" defeats winter in a dramatic performance with the enthusiastic participation of the public. In token of her victory, straw masks of the wicked winter giant are burned. The stage for this spectacle is represented by the houses of the suburb of Georgen, whose facades are lovingly decorated by their inhabitants with Binsenmark Easter eggs, roast cockerels and pretzels. Easter may indeed be the oldest Christian festival, but almost all the customs – at least in the Federal Republic of Germany – go back to old Germanic rites of worship centering on Ostara, the goddess of spring. The traditions connected with Easter rabbits, artificial Easter eggs, Easter fires and the healing power of water freed from the ice can be found almost everywhere. The Catholic part of the Sorbs, a Slavic farming minority settled in the Oberlausitz with an abundance of customs and splendid costumes still in lively use today, has retained an unusual Easter custom. In the "Easter ride" the men ride in frock-coats and top hats on festively decorated horses, to the ringing of bells and singing choruses through the streets lined with onlookers from parish to parish. This impressive demonstration of Sorbian religiosity was possible in the days of the GDR only when adapted to a socio-political level. Even the technique of colouring Easter eggs among the Sorbs is unique. In several processes, wax is applied to those parts of the eggs on which the colours are not supposed to adhere. This gives rise to the wonderfully beautiful ornaments for which Sorbian folk art is renowned.

In the Harz Mountains whose highest peak, the Brocken, is known as the mythical meeting place of the witches, on the night of 30 April/1 May, *Walpurgisnacht,* a witches' fire burns in many places, by the light of which the spookily masked devil addresses his witches. But then the brave coachmen crack their whips and drive off the evil spirit. The May Queen ceremonially declares winter defeated and opens the dance.

Concepts of reawakening fruitfulness in the coming spring are also connected with setting up the maypole on 1 May, and naturally the lads of the village make sure that their maypole is not stolen from them, while at the same time they do all they can to steal the maypole from the neighbouring village. In the area of Bad Berka in Thuringia the traditional "May polling" has been retained on Midsummer Day. In a merry procession, with the performance of a May play and the choice of a May Queen who leads the evening dance, the felling of the Maypole is celebrated.

The people of the Harz take part in their "Finch manoeuvres" at Whitsun, because finch-breeding is an old custom there. Under the expert eyes of the many spectators the breeders decide which cock finch is the most tenacious and melodious songster.

In farming areas, spring, summer and the beginning of autumn are filled with work – interrupted only by the midsummer celebrations, which are naturally at their most beautiful in the mountains, when in the evenings the fires flicker on the peaks. But in the autumn, at the consecration ceremony, harvest festival, and when the cattle are driven down from the mountain pastures, celebrations and customs are once more the focus of country life. A unique harvest festival is the "Hüttenrod Grass Dance". On that day the little town is firmly in the hands of the women and the men can take part only at their invitation. This custom arose at a time when the women had to bring in the harvest all alone because their husbands were working in the local mines. Led by their Grass Queen, they process to the festival place, where they celebrate boisterously.

In November people remember their dead and decorate the cemeteries, to experience reconciliation and peace in the face of autumn's glory of flowers. Yes – and a little later, the preparations for the most beautiful celebration of the year, Christmas, begin everywhere. The season of Advent, St. Nicholas' Day – the children's festival on 6 December – and Christmas Eve with all their customs and old traditions govern life in town and country. And when the Christmas or Christ's Markets in Hamburg, Dresden, Cologne, Nuremberg, Munich, Leipzig, Berlin and thousands of smaller towns and communities open their gates, when the fragrance of gingerbread hearts and nut biscuits, of Christmas fruitloaves and hot punch wafts down streets and across squares, and when the festive sound of trumpets rings out from the church towers, then the year is drawing to a close.

Besides the country and ecclesiastical festivities with their splendour and their customs, we must not forget the great historical celebrations, which almost all take place in the South German area. Here the days of remembrance of historical events are generally observed with theatrical performances and festive processions. For instance, in Landshut the "Landshut Princely Wedding" in memory of the marriage of Prince George the Rich approximately five hundred years ago is celebrated every three years with a historically faithful procession. Seesen is transposed by its inhabitants into centuries long past at the "Sehusafest". Noblemen, citizens and farmers in traditional authentic costumes give new life to scenes from the turbulent history of the thousand year-old little town. With mercenary foot-soldiers' camps on the torchlit market square, Renaissance dances and the dramatic representation of the "Seesen marriage" of 1592, they celebrate this festival, whose colourful culminating point is a mediaeval knights' tournament. In Dinkelsbühl, too, at the celebration of the "Kinderzeche", the citizens, dressed in historical costumes, recall a children's delegation during the Thirty Years War, which is said to have asked the Swedes for mercy for their town.

The most famous of all historical festivals, however, is the Munich *Oktoberfest,* to which visitors come from all over the world, to drink the light, sweet beer brewed specially for the occasion and to consume crisp chicken, delicious skewered fish fried over an open fire, and other delicacies. They stroll past the showmen's attractions and enjoy the nervous thrill on the amusement rides. The first *Oktoberfest* in 1810, however, looked quite different. At that time, King Max Joseph invited the citizens to a festival on the edge of town to celebrate the marriage of Crown Prince Ludwig to Princess Therese of Sachsen-Hildburghausen. This celebration was such a success that the Guards cavalry made the request to name the festival meadow after the bride, and the city of Munich decided to repeat the festival every year. And because on the occasion of the wedding the people of Munich marched past the Residence to the festival meadow in a festive procession, it is still the custom to organize a costume and festival procession through the city of Munich, which with its wealth of colour and variety remains an unforgettable experience for everyone who attends it, because groups in traditional costume arrive from all over the country. And the occasion may remind many people of Schiller's words: "There is a deep meaning immanent in the old customs; one must honour them."

Stefan Elsberger

Heidelberg on the banks of the Neckar in Baden-Württemberg is a romantic attraction for tourists from all over the world – especially during the annual illumination of the castle with a great display of fireworks.

Colourful processions – the picture shows Rottweil in Baden-Württemberg – are part of the Swabian-Alemannic Shrove Tuesday celebrations. Here a traditional "Federhannes" in his white feathered costume shows off his clownish tricks.

The strongholds of the Rhineland carnival are the cities of Cologne and Düsseldorf in North Rhine-Westphalia and Mainz in Rhineland-Palatinate. Above, the "Düxer Clowns" in the Cologne carnival procession: below, clowns on Düsseldorf's main street, the Königsallee.

Carnival strongholds in the new Federal *Länder* are Radeburg in Saxony or (illustrated) Wasungen in the Werra in Thuringia. The photograph shows an example of the famous "Manebacher Masks".

The "Sehusafest" in Seesen transposes the inhabitants of the little Harz township into past centuries.

The biggest German folk festival, on the turf of the Theresienwiese in Munich, is significant to the tourist trade. The "Oktoberfest" takes place every year at the end of September and attracts huge numbers of visitors, as do the other large and small folk festivals throughout the country, e. g. the Cannstatt *Wasen,* Bremen *Freimarkt,* the Annaberg *Kät,* the *Wiesenmarkt* in Eisleben, the Dresden *Vogelwiese,* the Weimar *Zwiebelmarkt* and the Hamburg *Dom.*

Right: community concert by the festival bands before the statue of Bavaria on the edge of the Munich Theresienwiese: below: bird's-eye view of the *Oktoberfest.*

The old shipping town of Cologne-Mülheim celebrates Corpus Christi with a traditional procession of ships on the Rhine, the "Mülheimer Gottestracht". From the banks and bridges thousands watch the journey of the ship of the sacrament *Cecilie* (foreground) and the accompanying ships of the "White Fleet".

The "Landshut Princely Wedding 1475" is one of the greatest historical entertainment events of Europe. Every four years the citizens of the town re-enact the Middle Ages for several weeks to recall the marriage of the Polish King's daughter, Hedwig (Jadwiga), with the Bavarian Duke's son, Georg.

For winter sports enthusiasts who do not want to go without their hobby even in the socalled "fifth season", there are the "Schnabler Races" in the Bavarian alpine foothills – above, a photograph from Gaissach. The picture below shows the Ski Carnival on the Firstalm on the lakeside of the Spitzingsee.

Ceremonial cattle-drive down from the alpine pastures in Upper Bavaria: of course, the cattle are adorned for their journey to winter quarters only if the herd has passed the summer on the mountain pastures without incident.

The North and Baltic Sea coasts, with their off-shore islands and more than a hundred landing places for fishing smacks, exert a special attraction for the inhabitants of the mainland. At the beginning and end of the fishing season there are festivals in many places. Our picture shows fishing smacks "dressed overall", with guests on board.

The Sorbian minority in the Lausitz celebrates the "Marriage of the Birds" on 25 January. Children dress up in picturesque wedding costumes and hope for presents.

The "Easter Ride" also offers an opportunity for putting on the old costumes. A typical one is the *"Borta"*, a top hat with an open top and with velvet trimming.

For the annual festival of the "Summer Victory" the inhabitants of Eisenach in Thuringia decorate their houses.

Sorbian women painting eggs: the egg, as an ancient symbol of fruitfulness is also, in Sorbian folk culture, a fixed feature of the Easter spring invocations.

Epiphany carol singing: an old Christmastide custom recalling the journey of the Three Kings. In earlier days, the donations collected went to unemployed craftsmen and to soldiers without work or pay: nowadays they go to charitable church funds, often for the Third World.

During the pre-Christmas period, the fragrance of fresh gingerbread and mulled wine drifts through the centres of German towns. On the right, St. Nicholas at the Nuremberg "Christ-Child Market": below, the Christmas Market on the Zeil in Frankfurt/Main.

The signing of the German-American Fulbright Agreement in 1952 by John McCloy, High Commissioner in Germany, and Federal Chancellor Konrad Adenauer. Under the terms of this programme – called after its initiator J. W. Fulbright, Senator from Arkansas – the two countries continue to exchange university students, professors and teachers as scholarship holders.

Exchange and Encounter

Since for non-German readers of this brochure the information on opportunities of coming into active contact with German culture will often be limited, we shall give some useful items of information here instead of general considerations. We shall restrict ourselves to the most important institutions, which, supported by public funds, assume the responsibility for cultural and information policy abroad, for scholarly exchange and development policy, and which constitute the Association for International Cooperation (VIZ).

For almost 40 years an annual Nobel prizewinners' meeting has been taking place in Lindau on Lake Constance. Apart from a changing number of laureates, there are also scholars, students, and interested members of the public taking part in the meetings. In the summer of 1988, there were 27 Nobel prizewinners and about 60 students and young scholars. Our picture shows the President of the Conference, Countess Sonja Bernadotte, with (from left to right) physicists Johannes Bednorz (Federal Republic of Germany), Heinrich Rohrer (Switzerland), Gerd Binnig (Federal Republic of Germany), and Karl Müller (Switzerland).

Alexander von Humboldt-Stiftung (AvH)
Jean-Paul-Strasse 12, D-5300 Bonn 2, Telephone (02 28) 8 33-0

The AvH awards one to two-year research grants to highly qualified scholars and scientists of foreign nationality and from every field to carry out research projects of their choice in the Federal Republic of Germany. The research grant is initially awarded for one year but an extension to a maximum of two years may be applied for. The amount of the monthly payments varies according to scientific qualification between DM 3,000 and 3,800. The follow-up programme (renewed short stays in Germany, donations of scientific instruments and specialized literature, foreign colloquia of the foundation and expert symposia, etc.) contributes to maintaining and intensifying the scholarly contacts with German science of more than 14,000 scholars previously sponsored.

In further programmes the AvH also awards up to 200 research prizes to internationally-known foreign scientists and up to 200 research grants annually to young German scientists holding doctorates who as a matter of principle go on to institutes of former Humboldt guest scientists abroad.

Annual Conference of the Humboldt Foundation in July of 1988 in Bonn: the Federal President, Richard von Weizsäcker, receiving the Humboldt guest scholars in the garden of the Villa Hammerschmidt.

Participants in the Carl Duisberg Society's programme for women secretaries in New York. Gaby Springer (left) and Gretel Flory visiting a television studio.

Carl Duisberg-Gesellschaft e. V. (CDG)
Hohenstaufenring 30–32, D-5000 Köln 1, Telephone (0221) 2098-0

The Carl Duisberg Society is a non-profit-making organization for international professional further training and personnel development. Its programmes are directed at skilled workers and executives from the Federal Republic of Germany and other industrialized countries as well as qualified employees and executives from developing countries. The CDG sees international professional further training as an important means of mutual stimulation of societies and cultures, of disseminating new ideas, and of launching processes of change and development. Here the professional further training of foreigners in Germany or of Germans abroad constitutes a part of development policy, of the foreign cultural policy, or educational policy. It may also be part of the foreign trade policy or foreign commitments of German enterprises.

The CDG derives its name from the chemist and entrepreneur Carl Duisberg (1861–1935), who after the First World War promoted visits to America for hundreds of German students as trainees in American companies on a work-study programme.

Deutsche Stiftung für internationale Entwicklung (DSE)
Rauchstrasse 25, D-1000 Berlin 30, Telephone (0 30) 26 06-1

The German Foundation for International Development (DSE) was founded in 1960 by the Federal Government and the *Länder* as a civil-law foundation in Berlin. Since then the DSE has been making a significant contribution to staff cooperation between the Federal Republic of Germany and the countries of the Third World. By means of dialogue and further education, the DSE supports the economic and social development of the countries in Africa, Asia, and Latin America.

Since 1960 the DSE, in collaboration with national and international partner organizations, has given more than 70,000 qualified employees and executives from more than 100 countries the opportunity to exchange their experiences on questions of international development and to acquire career-orientated further education. The main emphasis is on promoting rural development, safeguarding the supply of nutrition, and expanding commercial training facilities. In addition to this, the DSE supports measures to strengthen the planning and organizational capacity of the developing countries in administration, the health service, and the educational system. Special emphasis is put on self-help programmes for overcoming poverty.

The conference centre Villa Borsig, on Reiherwerder, houses the headquarters of the DSE. Since 1960, more than 30,000 qualified employees and executives from developing countries have discussed questions of international cooperation here and have been preparing for future tasks in their own countries in seminars of further education.

A view of the redesigned offices of the IfA-Library, which was re-opened in May 1988 after a two-year reconstruction period.

Institut für Auslandsbeziehungen (IfA)
Charlottenplatz 17, D-7000 Stuttgart 1, Telephone (0711) 2 22 50,
Telex 723772

The IfA is a public institution which promotes international cultural relations with all suitable media on the basis of mutuality. Among the many and varied activities of the Institute special mention should be made of: the organization of German art exhibitions to be shown abroad; the presentation of foreign art in the institute-owned "Forum for Cultural Exchange" and the "IfA Gallery" in Bonn, as well as of art from the former GDR and other Eastern European states through the Berlin exhibition service in the "Galerie Friedrichstrasse"; the publication of the "Journal for Cultural Exchange" which is dedicated to contemporary themes of cultural policy, and of publications on contemporary literature of other countries and the study of foreign countries; the organization of international symposia; the public relations work for the Federal Republic abroad in collaboration with the press and information service of the Federal Government; the organization of seminars on the study of Germany and foreign countries; advisory services for emigrants and people working abroad in a special advisory centre. Apart from these, the IfA has at its disposal the largest specialist library on the study of foreign countries and a well-stocked photographic library.

Goethe-Institut zur Pflege der deutschen Sprache im Ausland
und zur Förderung der internationalen kulturellen Zusammenarbeit e. V.
Lenbachplatz 3, D-8000 München 2, Telephone (0 89) 5 99 91

The Goethe Institute for the Cultivation of the German Language Abroad and for the Promotion of International Cultural Cooperation is a non-profit-making organization. Its tasks are: the provision and promotion of German teaching at home and abroad; collaboration with educational administrations, institutions, and teachers abroad; academic promotion of foreign teachers of German and Germanists; development and improvement of teaching methods and material; the awarding of grants for learning the German language and for the training and advanced training of foreign teachers of German; the organization and mediation of cultural events abroad; the communication of information abroad on cultural life in the Federal Republic of Germany; collaboration with cultural and scientific institutions abroad. Of particular interest are the focal points of the work of the 139 cultural institutes and 9 branch offices in 68 countries of the world: the teaching of German; involvement in the education and advanced training of German teachers abroad; seminars, symposia, and lectures by scientists and publicists; readings and workshops with artists and writers; theatre tours, guest directorships and festivals; chamber music tours and festivals; courses and seminars in musical education; jazz and pop tours; cultural information through films, videos, slides, photographs, books, texts, newspapers, tapes, and records; film shows, film weeks, and film festivals; film, television and radio seminars and workshops, some with film-makers and film and media specialists; documentation, photographic and art exhibitions; foundation and management of libraries and media libraries; despatch of books, specialist journals, slides, tapes, films, and records.

Information programme of the Goethe Institute in Schwäbisch Hall. Weekend on a ▶ farm for participants who seek first-hand information on problems of German agriculture.

Students of German at the Goethe Institutes in Schwäbisch Hall and Murnau: on the flight of steps at Schwäbisch Hall's Goethe Institute (left) and on an art expedition in front of the Gabriele-Münter-House in Murnau (right).

The DAAD awards several hundred grants annually to German and foreign students of art and music. German applicants present themselves in Bonn before a selection committee (picture).

Deutscher Akademischer Austauschdienst e. V. (DAAD)
Kennedyallee 50, D-5300 Bonn 2, Telephone (02 28) 88 20

The German Academic Exchange Service is a self-governing organization of the universities in the Federal Republic of Germany and Berlin (West) and is committed to promoting international relations between universities, especially academic and scientific exchanges. The DAAD maintains branch offices in Cairo, London, Nairobi, New Delhi, New York, Paris, Rio de Janeiro, San José (Costa Rica), and Tokyo. In 1964 an office was set up in Berlin to organize its programmes in Berlin (West), especially the artists' programme.

The artists' programme arose from the Artists in Residence Programme, founded 25 years ago by the Ford Foundation, and was intended to help protect Berlin (West) from the threatening cultural isolation. Since 1965 the programme has been run by the DAAD and the Senate of the city of Berlin (West) and annually brings 20 to 25 guests to the city on the banks of the Spree for one year: artists, composers, writers, and film-makers.

Inter Nationes e. V. (IN)
Kennedyallee 91–103, D-5300 Bonn 2, Telephone (0228) 8800

The registered association Inter Nationes has its headquarters in Bonn and, as an intermediary organization, works to increase knowledge of the Federal Republic of Germany for a better understanding of Germany abroad. In order to present a comprehensive picture of the cultural, social, economic and political life in this country, films, video tapes, sound tapes, records, books, posters and journals are produced, promoted, or bought for distribution. Feature films, television plays and documentaries are made available for film weeks, for the work of German agencies abroad, and for cultural institutes as well as for television stations. Inter Nationes provides information about cultural activity in the Federal Republic of Germany by means of books, brochures, journals and posters. A translation programme fosters the publication of German belles lettres and scientific specialist literature as well as of nonfiction and children's books in foreign languages. On behalf of the Federal Government, Inter Nationes organizes information tours through the Federal Republic of Germany for foreign journalists, politicians and representatives of cultural professions. The visitors' service maintains contact offices in Munich, Hamburg and Frankfurt am Main.

Group of visitors in front of the Inter Nationes building in Bonn.

Appendix

Supplementary Addresses

Literature

Bayerische Staatsbibliothek, Ludwigstraße 16, W-8000 München 22

Bibliothek des Deutschen Literaturarchivs/Schiller-Nationalmuseum, Schillerhöhe 8, W-7142 Marbach

Börsenverein der Deutschen Buchhändler zu Leipzig, Gerichtsweg 26, O-7010 Leipzig

Börsenverein des Deutschen Buchhandels e. V., Großer Hirschgraben 17–21, W-6000 Frankfurt 1

Deutsche Akademie der Künste (Ost), Otto-Kuschke-Straße 22/23, O-1080 Berlin

Deutsche Akademie für Sprache und Dichtung, Alexanderweg 23, W-6100 Darmstadt

Deutsche Bibliothek, Zeppelinallee 4–8, W-6000 Frankfurt 1

Deutsche Bücherei, Deutscher Platz, O-7010 Leipzig 1

Deutsche Staatsbibliothek, Unter den Linden 8, O-1080 Berlin

Deutscher Autoren-Verband e. V., Sophienstraße 2, W-3000 Hannover 1

Deutsches Literaturarchiv/Schiller-Nationalmuseum, Schillerhöhe 8, W-7142 Marbach

Gesellschaft für deutsche Sprache e. V., Taunusstraße 11, W-6200 Wiesbaden

Gutenberg-Museum der Stadt Mainz, Weltmuseum der Druckkunst, Liebfrauenplatz 5, W-6500 Mainz

Institut für deutsche Sprache, Friedrich-Karl-Straße 12, W-6800 Mannheim 1

Nationale Forschungs- und Gedenkstätten der klassischen deutschen Literatur in Weimar, Frauentorstraße 4, O-5300 Weimar

P. E. N.-Zentrum Bundesrepublik Deutschland, Sandstraße 10, W-6100 Darmstadt

Staatsbibliothek Preußischer Kulturbesitz, Potsdamer Straße 33, W-1000 Berlin 30

Verband deutscher Schriftsteller (VS) in der Industriegewerkschaft Druck und Papier, Friedrichstraße 15, W-7000 Stuttgart 1

Fine Arts

AICA: Internationaler Kunstkritikverband, Sektion der Bundesrepublik Deutschland, Maternusstraße 29, W-5000 Köln 1

Arbeitsgemeinschaft der Kunstbibliotheken, Germanisches Nationalmuseum (Bibliothek), Kornmarkt 1, W-8500 Nürnberg 11

Berliner Künstlerprogramm des Deutschen Akademischen Austauschdienstes (DAAD), Steinplatz 2, W-1000 Berlin 12

Bundesverband Bildender Künstler, Bundesgeschäftsstelle, Poppelsdorfer Allee 43, W-5300 Bonn 1

Bundesverband des Deutschen Kunst- und Antiquitätenhandels, Yorkstraße Nr. 11, W-3000 Hannover

Bundesverband Deutscher Galerien, St.-Apern-Straße 17, W-5000 Köln 1

Bundesverband Deutscher Kunstversteigerer, Neumarkt 3 (Kunsthaus Lempertz), W-5000 Köln 1

Deutscher Kunststudenten-Verband, Am Schloßgarten 3, W-5000 Köln 41 documenta und Museum Fridericianum Veranstaltungs-GmbH, Friedrich-Engels-Straße 20, W-3500 Kassel

Forum Bildender Künstler, Alfredistraße 2, W-4300 Essen

Gesellschaft für Bildende Kunst, Palais Walderdorff, Domfreiheit, W-5300 Trier

Gruppe RBK: Ring Bildender Künstler, Sedanstraße 68–68 a (Röderhaus), W-5600 Wuppertal 2

IGBK: Internationale Gesellschaft der Bildenden Künste, Sektion der Bundesrepublik Deutschland e. V., Poppelsdorfer Allee 43, W-5300 Bonn 1

Institut für moderne Kunst, Königstraße 51, W-8500 Nürnberg 1

Museums and Exhibitions

Deutscher Museumsbund, Erbprinzenstraße 13, W-7500 Karlsruhe 1

ICOM: The International Council of Museums – Internationaler Museumsrat, Deutsches Nationalkomitee, Museumsinsel 1 (Deutsches Museum), W-8000 München 26

Institut für Museumskunde, In der Halde Nr. 1, W-1000 Berlin 33

Zentralinstitut für Kunstgeschichte, Meiserstraße 10, W-8000 München 2

Theatre

ASSITEJ e. V., Internationale Vereinigung der Theater für Kinder und Jugendliche, Sektion Bundesrepublik Deutschland, Schützenstraße 12, W-6000 Frankfurt 1

ASSITEJ e. V., Internationale Vereinigung der Theater für Kinder und Jugendliche, Sektion Ost Am Stadtpark Nr. 2–3, O-1156 Berlin

Bund der Theatergemeinden e. V., Bonner Talweg 10, W-5300 Bonn 1

Bund deutscher Amateurtheater, Waiblinger Weg 12, W-7920 Heidenheim

Deutsche Akademie der Darstellenden

Künste e. V., Neue Mainzer Straße 19, W-6000 Frankfurt

Deutsche Shakespeare-Gesellschaft, Markt 13, O-5300 Weimar

Deutsche Theatertechnische Gesellschaft, Nobelstraße 37, W-5090 Leverkusen 1

Deutscher Bühnenverein, Bundesverband Deutscher Theater, Quatermarkt Nr. 5, W-5000 Köln 1

Deutsches Theatermuseum, Galeriestraße 4 a und 6, W-8000 München 22

Dramaturgische Gesellschaft e. V., Tempelhofer Ufer 22, W-1000 Berlin 61

Eurokultur Ost, Verein zur Förderung des kulturellen Austauschs mit den Ländern Osteuropas, Langhoffstraße 20, O-1140 Berlin

Genossenschaft Deutscher Bühnen-Angehöriger (GDBA), Feldbrunnenstraße 74, W-2000 Hamburg 13

Märkisches Museum, Theatersammlung, Am Köllnischen Park 5, O-1020 Berlin

Theatergeschichtliche Sammlung und Hebbel-Sammlung, Dänische Straße 15, W-2300 Kiel

Theatermuseum des Instituts für Theater-, Film- und Fernsehwissenschaft der Universität zu Köln, Schloß Wahn, W-5000 Köln 90

Theatermuseum Porz, Schloß, W-5050 Porz

Verband der deutschen Kritiker e. V., Gerviniusstraße 11, W-1000 Berlin 12

Verband der deutschen Volksbühnen-Vereine e. V., Am Handelshof 9, W-4300 Essen 1

Verband Deutscher Bühnenverleger e. V., Bismarckstraße 107, W-1000 Berlin 12

Verband Deutscher Freilichtbühnen e. V., – Region Nord –, Bankerheide 4, W-4700 Hamm 1

Verband Deutscher Freilichtbühnen e. V., – Region Süd –, Schillerstraße 18, W-7447 Aichtal

Zentrum Bundesrepublik Deutschland des Internationalen Theater-Instituts e. V., Bismarckstraße 107, W-1000 Berlin 12

Zentrum für Theaterforschung/Hamburger Theatersammlung, Von-Melle-Park Nr. 3, W-2000 Hamburg 13

Music

AG Song, Arbeitsgemeinschaft der Liedermacherinnen und Liedermacher aus der Bundesrepublik Deutschland, Mailänder Straße 14/92, W-6000 Frankfurt 70

Arbeitsgemeinschaft Deutscher Chorverbände, Bernhardstraße 166, W-5000 Köln 51

Arbeitskreis Musikpädagogischer Seminare in der Bundesrepublik Deutschland, Hochschule für Musik und Theater, Emmichplatz 1, W-3000 Hannover

Deutsche Jazz-Föderation e. V., Kleine Bockenheimer Straße 12, W-6000 Frankfurt

Deutsche Orchestervereinigung e. V. in der DAG, Heimbuderstraße 5, W-2000 Hamburg 13

Deutscher Komponisten-Verband, Beukestraße 26, W-1000 Berlin 37

Deutscher Musikrat – Sektion Bundesrepublik Deutschland im Internationalen Musikrat, Am Michaelshof 4 a, W-5300 Bonn 2

Deutscher Musikverband, Besenbinderhof 60, W-2000 Hamburg 1

Deutsches Volksliederarchiv, Arbeitsstelle für internationale Volksliedforschung, Silberbachstraße 13, W-7800 Freiburg

Dresdner Gesellschaft der Musikfreunde e. V., Schützenhofstraße 8, O-8023 Dresden

Forschungsinstitut für Musiktheater, Universität Bayreuth, W-8656 Schloß Turnau

GEMA: Gesellschaft für musikalische Aufführungs- und mechanische Vervielfältigungsrechte, Bayreuther Straße 37–38, W-1000 Berlin 30

Gemeinschaft Deutscher Musikverbände, Friedrich-Wilhelm-Straße 31, W-5300 Bonn 1

Gesellschaft für Musikforschung e. V., Heinrich-Schütz-Allee 35, W-3500 Kassel-Wilhelmshöhe

IG Medien, Am Michaelkirchplatz 4, O-1020 Berlin

Institut für Neue Musik und Musikerziehung e. V., Grafenstraße 35, W-6100 Darmstadt

Internationale Vereinigung der Musikbibliotheken – Deutsche Gruppe –, Salvatorplatz 1, W-8000 München 2

Internationaler Arbeitskreis für Musik e. V., Heinrich-Schütz-Allee 29, W-3500 Kassel-Wilhelmshöhe

Internationales Musikinstitut Darmstadt (IMD), Informationszentrum für zeitgenössische Musik, Nieder-Ramstädter Straße 190, W-6100 Darmstadt

Kontakt- und Informationsbüro für Vereinigungen und Verbände des künstlerischen Volksschaffens, Dietrichring 4, O-7010 Leipzig

Kulturamt der Stadt Dessau, Dezernat Bildung, Kultur, Tourismus, Rathaus, O-4500 Dessau

Kulturamt der Stadt Dresden, Dezernat für Kultur und Tourismus, Dr.-Külz-Ring 19, O-8010 Dresden

Kulturamt der Stadt Leipzig, Kulturdezernat, Neues Rathaus, O-7010 Leipzig

Kulturamt der Hansestadt Rostock, Kröpeliner Straße 25, O-2500 Rostock

Kulturamt der Stadt Weimar, Rathaus, O-5300 Weimar

Musikinstrumenten-Museum des Staatlichen Instituts für Musikforschung, Tiergartenstraße 1, W-1000 Berlin 30

Musikinstrumentensammlung der Universität Erlangen, Bismarckstraße 1, W-8520 Erlangen

Rektorenkonferenz der Staatlichen Musikhochschule, Dagobertstraße 38, W-5000 Köln 1

Stiftung Kulturfonds, Molkenmarkt 1–3, O-1020 Berlin

Verband Deutscher Komponisten e. V., An der Kolonnade 15, O-1080 Berlin

Verband deutscher Musikschulen e. V., Villichgasse 17, W-5300 Bonn 2

Arts and Crafts

Angermuseum, Am Anger 18, O-5010 Erfurt

Bayerisches Nationalmuseum, Prinzregentenstraße 3, W-8000 München 22

Bundesinnungsverband des Deutschen Steinmetz-, Stein- und Holzbildhauer-handwerks, Am Hirtenacker 47, W-6000 Frankfurt 90

Bundesinnungsverband für das Musik-instrumenten-Handwerk, Scheide-mannplatz 2, W-3500 Kassel

Bundesverband Kunsthandwerk e. V., Bleichstraße 36, W-6000 Frankfurt

Die Neue Sammlung, Staatliches Museum für angewandte Kunst, Prinzregentenstraße 3, W-8000 München 22

Geigenbau- und Heimatmuseum Mittenwald, Ballenhausgasse 3, W-8102 Mittenwald

Germanisches Nationalmuseum, Kornmarkt 1, W-8500 Nürnberg

Gesellschaft für Goldschmiedekunst, Deutsches Goldschmiedehaus, Altstädter Markt 6, W-6450 Hanau

Gewerbemuseum Nürnberg, Gewerbemuseumsplatz 2, W-8500 Nürnberg

Hochschule für industrielle Formgestaltung, Burg Giebichenstein, O-4020 Halle

Kunstgewerbemuseum Berlin, Schloß Köpenick, Schloßinsel, O-1170 Berlin

Kunstsammlung zu Weimar, Burgplatz 4, O-5300 Weimar

Museum des Kunsthandwerks, Johannisplatz, O-7000 Leipzig

Museum für Angewandte Kunst (Kunstgewerbemuseum), An der Rechtschule, W-5000 Köln 1

Museum für Deutsche Volkskunde SMDK, Im Winkel 6/8, W-1000 Berlin 33

Museum für Kunsthandwerk, Schloß Pillnitz, O-8054 Dresden

Museum für Kunst und Gewerbe, Steintorplatz 1, W-2000 Hamburg 1

Staatliche Galerie Moritzburg, Friedemann-Bach-Platz 5, O-4020 Halle

Verband deutscher Geigenbauer Stuttgart e. V., Kernerstraße 37, W-7000 Stuttgart 1

Zentralverband des Deutschen Handwerks, Johanniterstraße 1, W-5300 Bonn 1

Zentralverband für das Juwelier-, Gold- und Silberschmiede-Handwerk, Contrescarpe 63, W-2800 Bremen 1

Architecture and Preservation of Historic Monuments

Arbeitskreis Theorie und Lehre der Denkmalpflege, Vorsitz: Aufbaustudium Denkmalpflege, An der Universität 2, W-8600 Bamberg.

BDA: Bund Deutscher Architekten, Bundessekretariat, Ippendorfer Allee 14 b, W-5300 Bonn 1

BDB: Bund Deutscher Baumeister, Architekten und Ingenieure e. V., Berliner Freiheit 16, W-5300 Bonn 1

BDLA: Bund Deutscher Landschaftsarchitekten e. V., Colmantstraße 32, W-5300 Bonn 1

Bundesarchitektenkammer, Holbeinstraße 17, W-5300 Bonn 2

Deutsche Akademie für Städtebau und Landesplanung, Kaiserplatz 4, W-8000 München 40

Deutsche UNESCO-Kommission, Colmantstraße 15, W-5300 Bonn 1

Deutsches Nationalkomitee für Denkmalschutz beim Bundesminister des Innern, Graurheindorfer Straße 198, W-5300 Bonn 1

Deutsches Nationalkomitee von ICO-MOS, Geschäftsstelle: Bayerisches Landesamt für Denkmalpflege, Hofgraben 4, W-8000 München 22

Koordinierungs- und Beratungsstelle für Umweltschäden an Denkmälern, Umweltbundesamt, Bismarckplatz 1, W-1000 Berlin 33

Vereinigung der Landesdenkmalpfleger in der Bundesrepublik Deutschland, Geschäftsstelle: Kulturbehörde Hamburg, Denkmalamt, Imstedt 18–20, W-2000 Hamburg 76

Design and Fashion

Art Directors Club e. V., Grabenstraße 2, W-4000 Düsseldorf

Akademie für das Graphische Gewerbe, Pranckhstraße 2, W-8000 München 2

Bauhaus Dessau, Thälmannallee 38, O-4500 Dessau

Design Center Stuttgart, Haus der Wirtschaft, Willi-Bleicher-Straße 19, W-7000 Stuttgart 10

Design Zentrum Dresden, Semperstraße
Nr. 15, O-8020 Dresden
Design Zentrum Hessen, Eugen-Bracht-
Weg 6, W-6100 Darmstadt
Design Zentrum München, Kaiserstraße
45, W-8000 München 40
Design Zentrum Nordrhein-Westfalen,
Hindenburgstraße 25–27, W-4300 Es-
sen 1
Deutsche Meisterschule für Mode, Roß-
markt 15, W-8000 München 2
Deutscher Designertag e. V., Kreuzberg-
straße 1, W-4000 Düsseldorf
Deutscher Werkbund e. V., Weißadler-
gasse 4, W-6000 Frankfurt 1
Deutsches Plakat Museum, Theaterpas-
sage, Rathenaustraße 2, W-4300 Essen
1
Informationsbulletin des VBK, Insel-
straße 12, O-1020 Berlin
Institut für neue technische Form e. V.,
Eugen-Bracht-Weg 6, W-6100 Darm-
stadt
Internationales Design Zentrum Berlin,
Kurfürstendamm 66, W-1000 Berlin
15
Neue Industriekultur, Clara-Zetkin-
Straße 28, O-1080 Berlin
Rat für Formgebung, Rat-Haus, Messe-
gelände, W-6000 Frankfurt/Main 1

Film and Television

Arbeitsgemeinschaft Neuer Deutscher
Film, Agnesstraße 14, W-8000 Mün-
chen 40
ARD: Arbeitsgemeinschaft der öffent-
lich-rechtlichen Rundfunkanstalten der
Bundesrepublik Deutschland, ARD-
Büro, Bertramstraße 8, W-6000 Frank-
furt 1
Bundesverband Deutscher Fernsehprodu-
zenten e. V., Widenmayerstraße 32, W-
8000 München 22
Bundesverband Deutscher Film- und AV-
Produzenten e. V., Langenbeckstraße
Nr. 9, W-6200 Wiesbaden
DEFA-Studio Babelsberg im Aufbau,
August-Bebel-Straße 26–53, O-1591
Potsdam
Deutsche Film- und Fernsehakademie,
Pommernallee 1, W-1000 Berlin 19

Deutscher Auslandsdienst für Rundfunk
und Fernsehen, Konstantinstraße 58,
W-5300 Bonn 2
Deutscher Fernsehfunk (DFF), Rudower
Chaussee 3, O-1199 Berlin
Deutsches Rundfunkarchiv (DRA), Ber-
tramstraße 8, W-6000 Frankfurt/Main 1
Eins Plus, Satellitenkanal der ARD, Pro-
grammdirektion Deutsches Fernsehen,
Arnulfstraße 42, W-8000 München 2
Filmbewertungsstelle Wiesbaden, Schloß
Biebrich, W-6200 Wiesbaden 12
Filmförderungsanstalt – Bundesanstalt
des öffentlichen Rechts –, Budapester
Straße 41, W-1000 Berlin 30
Filmmuseum Potsdam, Am Karl-Lieb-
knecht-Forum, O-1560 Potsdam
German Television News GmbH, GTN-
Studio am Corbusierhaus, W-1000
Berlin 19
Hauptverband Deutscher Filmtheater
e. V., Langenbeckstraße 19, W-6200
Wiesbaden
Hochschule für Fernsehen und Film,
Frankenthaler Straße 23, W-8000
München 90
Hochschule für Film und Fernsehen
"Konrad Wolf", Karl-Marx-Straße 27,
O-1591 Potsdam-Babelsberg
Progress-Filmverleih, Burgstraße 27, O-
1020 Berlin
PRO 7 Television GmbH, Bahnhofstraße
27a, W-8043 Unterföhring
RIAS-TV, Voltastraße 69, W-1000 Berlin
65
RTL plus Deutschland Fernsehen
GmbH & Co., Betriebs KG, Aachener
Straße Nr. 1036, W-5000 Köln 40
Sat Satellitenfernsehen des deutschen
Sprachraums (ZDF/ORF/SRG), Essen-
heimer Landstraße, W-6500 Mainz-
Lerchenberg
SAT 1 Satelliten Fernsehen GmbH, He-
gelstraße 61, W-6500 Mainz
Spitzenorganisation der Filmwirtschaft
e. V., Langenbeckstraße 9, W-6200
Wiesbaden
Sportkanal GmbH, Joseph-Dollinger-Bo-
gen 30, W-8000 München 40
Super Channel Ltd., Goethestraße 11/IV,
W-8000 München 2
TELE 5 Kabel-Media-Programmgesell-

schaft mbH, Schellingstraße 44, W-8000 München 40

TransTel, Gesellschaft für Deutsche Fernsehtranskription mbH, Raderberggürtel Nr. 50, W-5000 Köln 51

Verband der Filmverleiher e. V., Langenbeckstraße 9, W-6200 Wiesbaden

Verband Deutscher Spielfilmproduzenten e. V., Freystraße 4, W-8000 München 23

ZDF: Zweites Deutsches Fernsehen, Essenheimer Landstraße, W-6500 Mainz-Lerchenberg

Customs and Festivals

Bund der Historischen Deutschen Schützenbruderschaften e. V., Am Kreispark 22 (Friedberger Hof), W-5090 Leverkusen 3-Opladen

Bund Deutscher Karneval e. V., Vereinigung zur Pflege fastnachtlicher Bräuche, Postfach 13 68, W-5102 Würselen

Deutsche Gesellschaft für Freizeit e. V., Bahnhofstraße 4, W-4006 Erkrath

Deutsche Gesellschaft für Volkskunde e. V., Universität München, Ludwigstraße 25, W-8000 München 22

Deutscher Heimatbund e. V., Buschstraße 4, W-5300 Bonn 1

Deutscher Schaustellerbund e. V., Hochkreuzallee 67, W-5300 Bonn 2

Deutsches Fastnachtmuseum, Postfach Nr. 11, W-8710 Kitzingen

Institut für Volkskunde/Europäische Ethnologie, Humboldt-Universität, Friedenstraße 3, O-1017 Berlin

Verband Deutscher Heimat- und Volkstrachten-Vereine e. V., c/o Otto Kragler, Dorotheenstraße 21, W-8000 München 82

Exchange and Encounter

Arbeitsring Ausland für kulturelle Aufgaben e. V., Gustav-Heinemann-Ufer Nr. 84–88, W-5000 Köln 51

AvH: Alexander von Humboldt-Stiftung, Jean-Paul-Straße 12, W-5300 Bonn 2

CDG: Carl Duisburg Gesellschaft e. V., Hohenstaufenring 30–32, W-5000 Köln 1

DAAD: Deutscher Akademischer Austauschdienst, Kennedyallee 50, W-5300 Bonn 2

Deutsche Gesellschaft für die Vereinten Nationen e. V., Dag-Hammarskjöld-Haus, Poppelsdorfer Allee 55, W-5300 Bonn 1

Deutsche UNESCO-Kommission, Colmantstraße 15, W-5300 Bonn 1

Deutsches Komitee für kulturelle Zusammenarbeit in Europa e. V., Aloys-Schulte-Straße 6, W-5300 Bonn 1

DSE: Deutsche Stiftung für internationale Entwicklung, Hans-Böckler-Straße 5, W-5300 Bonn 3

Goethe-Institut zur Pflege der deutschen Sprache im Ausland und zur Förderung der internationalen kulturellen Zusammenarbeit e. V., Lenbachplatz 3, W-8000 München 1

Institut für Auslandsbeziehungen, Charlottenplatz 17, W-7000 Stuttgart 1

Institut für Internationale Begegnungen e. V., Walramstraße 9, W-5300 Bonn 2

Internationales Jugend-Kulturzentrum Bayreuth e. V., Postfach 26 03, W-8580 Bayreuth

Inter Nationes, Kennedyallee 91–103, W-5300 Bonn 2

Verein für Internationale Jugendarbeit e. V., Adenauerallee 37, W-5300 Bonn 1

Further Addresses

Archiv für Kulturpolitik ARCULT, Am Hofgarten 17, W-5300 Bonn 1

Deutsche Forschungsgemeinschaft, Kennedyallee 40, W-5300 Bonn 2

Gedok: Verband der Gemeinschaften der Künstlerinnen und Kunstfreunde e. V., Einern 29, D-5600 Wuppertal 2

Ständige Konferenz der Kultusminister der Länder in der Bundesrepublik Deutschland, Nassestraße 8, W-5300 Bonn 1

Verein zur Förderung von Kunst und Wissenschaft zu Bremen, Klattendick 18, W-2800 Bremen

Zentrum für Kulturforschung, Am Hofgarten 16, W-5300 Bonn 1

Supplementary Bibliography

Literature

Arnold, H.L. (Ed.): Bestandsaufnahme Gegenwartsliteratur. Edition Text + Kritik, Munich 1988.

Demetz, P.: Die süße Anarchie. Skizzen zur deutschen Literatur seit 1945. Ullstein, Frankfurt am Main 1973.

Emmerich, W.: Kleine Literaturgeschichte der DDR. Enlarged edition. Luchterhand, Frankfurt am Main 1989.

Hage, V.: Die Wiederkehr des Erzählers. Neue deutsche Literatur der siebziger Jahre. Ullstein, Frankfurt am Main 1982.

Thomas, R.H., K. Bullivant: Westdeutsche Literatur der sechziger Jahre. dtv, Munich 1975.

Winkels, H.: Einschnitte. Zur Literatur der 80er Jahre. Suhrkamp, Frankfurt am Main 1991.

Fine Arts

Altes Museum Berlin: Alltag und Epoche. Werke bildender Kunst der DDR aus 35 Jahren. Berlin 1984.

Arbeitsgemeinschaft deutscher Kunstvereine (Ed.): Kunstlandschaft Bundesrepublik. 11 vols. Stuttgart 1984.

Gillen, E., R. Haarmann (Ed.): Kunst in der DDR. Kiepenheuer & Witsch, Cologne 1990.

Guggenheim Museum (Ed.): Refigured Painting – The German Image 1960 to 1988. New York 1989.

Henkel, J., S. Russ (Ed.): Künstlerbücher und originalgrafische Zeitschriften im Eigenverlag. Merlin Verlag, Gifkendorf 1991.

Honnef, K. (Ed.): Zwischenbilanz II, Neue deutsche Kunst. Kunstforum International (Vol. 68), Cologne 1983.

Kuhirt, U. (Ed.): Kunst der DDR 1960 bis 1980. Seemann, Leipzig 1983.

Lang, L.: Malerei und Graphik in der DDR. Reclam, Leipzig 1978/1987.

Museumspädagogischer Dienst Berlin (Ed.): Kunstkombinat DDR – eine Dokumentation 1945–1990. With contributions by: Feist, G., E. Gillen et al. Verlag Dirk Nishen, Berlin 1990.

Nationalgalerie, Staatliche Museen Preußischer Kulturbesitz (Ed.): Kunst in der Bundesrepublik Deutschland 1945–1985. Berlin 1985.

Tannert, Ch. (Ed.): Autoperforationsartistik. Institut für moderne Kunst, Nuremberg 1991.

Thomas, K.: Zweimal deutsche Kunst nach 1945. DuMont, Cologne 1985.

Thomas, R., G. Muschter (Ed.): Jenseits der Staatskultur. Traditionen autonomer Kunst in der DDR. Carl Hanser Verlag, Munich 1992.

Verein der Freunde und Förderer des Hessischen Landesmuseums Darmstadt (Ed.): Tiefe Blicke – Kunst der 80er Jahre aus der BRD, der DDR, Österreich und der Schweiz. Cologne 1985.

Museums and Exhibitions

Arbeitsgemeinschaft deutscher Kunstvereine (Ed.): Kunstlandschaft Bundesrepublik. Klett Cotta, Stuttgart 1984.

Auer, H. (Ed.): Bewahren und Ausstellen. Die Förderung des kulturellen Erbes in Museen. Verlag K.G. Saur, Munich 1984.

Belser Kunst Quartal. Vierteljährliche Vorschau auf in- und ausländische Kunstausstellungen. Belser Verlag, Stuttgart 1965 ff.

Bott, G. (Ed.): Das Museum der Zukunft. DuMont, Cologne 1970.

Deutsche Forschungsgemeinschaft (Ed.): Zur Lage der Museen. Denkschrift, Bonn 1974.

Karlsruher Schriften zur Besucherforschung (in cooperation with: Institut für Museumskunde, Berlin). Institut für Soziologie der Universität Karlsruhe, Karlsruhe 1991 ff.

Mörmann, K. (Ed.): Der deutsche Museumsführer. Museen und Sammlungen in der Bundesrepublik Deutschland und West-Berlin. 3rd edition. Wolfgang Krüger Verlag, Frankfurt am Main 1986.

Schubert, H.: Moderner Museumsbau. Deutschland, Österreich, Schweiz. Deutsche Verlagsanstalt, Stuttgart 1986.

Theatre

100 Jahre Deutsches Theater Berlin 1883–1983. Henschel, Berlin 1983.

25 Jahre Theatertreffen Berlin (1964 bis 1988). Argon, Berlin 1988.

Baer, H.: Schlafen kann ich, wenn ich tot bin – Das atemlose Leben des Rainer Werner Fassbinder. Kiepenheuer & Witsch, Cologne 1982.

Canaris, V.: Peter Zadek – der Theatermann und Filmemacher. Carl Hanser Verlag, Munich 1979.

Carstensen, U. B.: Klaus Michael Grüber. Fischer, Frankfurt am Main 1988.

Gleber, K.: Theater und Öffentlichkeit. Produktions- und Rezeptionsbedingungen des politischen Theaters am Beispiel Piscators 1920–1966. Dissertation der Universität Tübingen, Tübingen 1979.

Goertz, H.: Gustaf Gründgens in Selbstzeugnissen und Bilddokumenten. Rowohlt, Reinbek bei Hamburg 1982.

Gründgens, G.: Briefe, Aufsätze, Reden. Hoffmann und Campe, Hamburg 1967.

Hensel, G.: Spiels noch einmal. Das Theater der achtziger Jahre. Suhrkamp, Frankfurt am Main 1990.

Hoffmann, L., K. Siebig: Ernst Busch. Eine Biographie in Texten, Bildern und Dokumenten. Henschel, Berlin 1987.

Iden, P.: Die Schaubühne am Halleschen Ufer 1970–1979. Carl Hanser Verlag, Munich 1979.

Kortner, F.: Aller Tage Abend. Kindler, Munich 1959.

Kranz, D.: Berliner Theater – 100 Aufführungen aus 3 Jahrzehnten. Henschel, Berlin 1990.

Lange, M.: Peter Zadek. Fischer, Frankfurt am Main 1989.

Lexikon der Festspiele. Rheinverlag, Pulheim 1984.

Mertz, P.: Das gerettete Theater – Die deutsche Bühne im Wiederaufbau. Quadriga, Weinheim 1990.

Mittenzwei, W.: Das Leben des Bertolt Brecht oder Der Umgang mit Welträtseln. Aufbau-Verlag, Berlin 1988.

Müller, H.: Krieg ohne Schlacht. Das Leben in zwei Diktaturen. Kiepenheuer & Witsch, Cologne 1992.

Neef, S.: Das Theater der Ruth Berghaus. Henschel, Berlin 1989.

Ohngemach, G.: George Tabori. Fischer, Frankfurt am Main 1989.

Piscator, E.: Briefe aus Deutschland 1951–1966. Prometh, Cologne 1983.

Pollow, H.: Interpretationen klassischer Dramentexte im Schauspieltheater der DDR während der siebziger und achtziger Jahre. Dissertation an der Humboldt-Universität, Berlin 1988.

Reichel, P.: Kontinuität und Diskontinuität in der DDR-Dramatik der achtziger Jahre. Dissertation an der Leipziger Universität, Leipzig 1988.

Schaubühne am Halleschen Ufer am Leniner Platz 1962–1987. Propyläen Verlag, Berlin 1987.

Schneider, R.: Theater in einem besiegten Land. Dramaturgie der deutschen Nachkriegszeit 1945–1949. Ullstein, Frankfurt am Main 1989.

Schumacher, E.: Berliner Kritiken. 3 vols. Henschel, Berlin 1975/1982.

Schumacher, E.: Brecht-Kritiken. Henschel, Berlin 1982.

Storch, W. (Ed.): Explosion of a Memory, Heiner Müller, DDR. Ein Arbeitsbuch. Edition Hentrich, Berlin 1988.

Theaterarbeit. 6 Aufführungen des Berliner Ensembles. 3rd ed. Henschel, Berlin 1967.

Tragelehn, B. K.: Theater-Arbeiten. Edition Hentrich, Berlin 1988.

Ulischberger, E.: Schauspiel in Dresden. Henschel, Berlin 1989.

Völker, K.: Fritz Kortner, Schauspieler und Regisseur. Edition Hentrich, Berlin 1987.

Wekwerth, M.: Schriften. Arbeit mit Brecht. Henschel, Berlin 1973.

Music

Belkins, G., U. Liedtke (Ed.): Musik für die Oper. Mit Komponisten im Gespräch. Henschel, Berlin 1990.

Burde, W. (Ed.): Aspekte der Neuen Musik. Bärenreiter, Kassel 1968.

Das Orchester. Schott, Mainz.

Döpfner, M. O. C., Th. Garms: Neue Deutsche Welle – Kunst oder Mode? Ullstein, Berlin 1984.

Fachblatt Musik-Magazin. Spezial Zeitschriften Verlag, Munich.

Flender, R., H. Rauhe (Ed.): Popmusik. Wissenschaftliche Buchgesellschaft, Darmstadt 1983.

Hopf, H., B. Sonntag (Ed.): Im Osten nichts Neues? Zur Musik der DDR. F. Noetzel, Wilhelmshaven 1989.

Kolleritsch, O. (Ed.): Oper heute. Formen der Wirklichkeit im zeitgenössischen Musiktheater. Universal Edition, Vienna 1985.

Metzger, H.-K., R. Riehn: Musik-Konzepte. Die Reihe über Komponisten. Edition Text + Kritik, Munich (6 vols. annually).

Motte, D. de la (Ed.): Neue Musik – Quo vadis? Schott, Mainz 1988.

Musik und Bildung. Schott, Mainz.

Neue Musikzeitung. Bosse, Regensburg.

Neue Zeitschrift für Musik. Schott, Mainz.

Rothschild, Th.: Liedermacher. 23 Porträts. Fischer, Frankfurt am Main 1980.

Stürzbecher, U.: Komponisten in der DDR. 17 Gespräche. Gerstenberg, Hildesheim 1979.

Wadenbeißer, B. (Ed.): Musik und Legeleistung. Fachverlag des oologischen Zentralinstituts der DDR, Berlin 1989.

Arts and Crafts

Arbeitsgemeinschaft des Kunsthandwerks in Hamburg e. V.: Kunsthandwerk in Hamburg. Christians Verlag, Hamburg 1980.

Deutsches Kunsthandwerk. Mitgliederverzeichnis. Bundesverband Kunsthandwerk e. V., Düsseldorf 1990.

Hoos, H.: Zeitgenössisches deutsches Kunsthandwerk. 3. Triennale 1984. Museum für Kunsthandwerk Frankfurt am Main/Kestner-Museum Hanover, Frankfurt am Main 1984.

Jahresschau des Schleswig-Holsteinischen Kunsthandwerks 1989. With contributions by: Fuchs-Belhamri, E., M. Koeppen, Ch. Rathke and H. Spielmann. Schleswig-Holsteinisches Landesmuseum Schloß Gottorf, Schleswig 1989.

Meister der deutschen Keramik. Katalog bearbeitet von: Reineking von Bock, G. Kunstgewerbemuseum Köln, Cologne 1978.

Modes, A.: Schönes Kunsthandwerk. Ein Streifzug durch Manufakturen, Epochen, Kulturen, Sammlungen. Thiemig, Munich 1985.

Runde, S. et al.: Zeitgenössisches deutsches Kunsthandwerk. 5. Triennale 1990/1991. Museum für Kunsthandwerk Frankfurt am Main/Grassi-Museum/Kestner-Museum Hanover. Prestel, Munich 1990.

Runde, S. et al.: Zeitgenössisches deutsches und finnisches Kunsthandwerk. 4. Triennale 1987/1988. Museum für Kunsthandwerk Frankfurt am Main/Taideteollisuusmuseo Helsinki/Kestner-Museum Hanover, Frankfurt am Main 1987.

Spielmann, H.: Kunsthandwerk aus Hamburg und Norddeutschland. Wanderausstellung Japan, Australien, China. Museum für Kunst und Gewerbe Hamburg, Hamburg 1985.

Zahle, E. (Ed.): Skandinavisches Kunsthandwerk. Droemer/Knaur, Munich 1963.

Architecture and Preservation of Historical Monuments

Arendt, C.: Altbau-Erneuerung. Leitfaden zur Erhaltung und Modernisierung alter Häuser. Deutsche Verlagsanstalt, Stuttgart 1977.

Berger, H. (Ed.): Baudenkmalpflege. Beiträge zur Methodik und Technologie. In: Institut für Denkmalpflege (Ed.): Schriften zur Denkmalpflege. Verlag für Bauwesen, Berlin 1990.

Bofinger, H., M. Bofinger, H. Klotz, J. Paul: Architektur in Deutschland: Bundesrepublik und Westberlin. Kohlhammer, Stuttgart 1981.

Denkmalpflege in der Bundesrepublik Deutschland. Geschichte, Organisation, Aufgaben, Beispiele. Ein Beitrag zum Europäischen Denkmalschutzjahr 1975. Inter Nationes/Moos Verlag, Bonn-Bad Godesberg/Gräfelfing 1982. Engl. ed.: The Conservation of Historical Monuments in the Federal Republic of Germany. History, Organisation, Tasks, Case-histories. Inter Nationes/ Moos Verlag, Bonn-Bad Godesberg/ Gräfelfing 1982. French ed.: La Conservation des Monuments en République Fédérale d'Allemagne. Historique, organisation, missions, exemples. Inter Nationes/Moos Verlag, Bonn-Bad Godesberg/Gräfelfing 1982.

Durth, W., N. Gutschow: Träume in Trümmern. Planungen zum Wiederaufbau zerstörter Städte im Westen Deutschlands 1940–1950. Vol. 1: Konzepte; Vol. 2: Städte. In: Schriften des Deutschen Architekturmuseums zur Architekturgeschichte und Architekturtheorie. Vieweg & Sohn, Braunschweig – Wiesbaden 1988.

Erhaltung, Erneuerung und Wiederbelebung alter Stadtgebiete in Europa. Gemeinsame europäische Kulturstudie im Auftrag des Bundesministers für Raumordnung, Bauwesen und Städtebau, Bonn; Deutsche UNESCO-Kommission, Bonn. Part 1: Die Situation in der Bundesrepublik Deutschland, p. 11 ff. In: Schriftenreihe "Stadtentwicklung" des Bundesministers für Raumordnung, Bauwesen und Städtebau, Bonn 1981.

Findeisen, P.: Geschichte der Denkmalpflege: Sachsen-Anhalt. Von den Anfängen bis in das erste Drittel des 20. Jahrhunderts. Verlag für Bauwesen, Berlin 1990.

Flagge, I. (Ed.): Industriebrachen. Vom Technologiepark bis zum Medienzentrum: Neue Chancen, neue Nutzungen. Im Auftrag des Ministers für Stadtentwicklung, Wohnen und Verkehr des Landes Nordrhein-Westfalen. Krämer (Architektur in der Demokratie 5), Stuttgart – Zurich 1990.

Gebessler, A., W. Eberl (Ed.): Schutz und Pflege von Baudenkmälern in der Bundesrepublik Deutschland. Kohlhammer, Stuttgart 1980.

Güttler, P., et al.: Berlin – Brandenburg. Ein Architekturführer – An Architectural Guide. (German/English) Ernst & Sohn, Berlin 1990.

Huse, N. (Ed.): Denkmalpflege. Deutsche Texte aus drei Jahrhunderten. C.H. Beck, Munich 1984.

Kieling, U., G. Priese et al. (Ed.): Historische Stadtkerne. Städte unter Denkmalschutz. VEB Tourist Verlag, Berlin – Leipzig 1990.

Magirius, H.: Geschichte der Denkmalpflege: Sachsen. Von den Anfängen bis zum Neubeginn 1945. Verlag für Bauwesen, Berlin 1989.

Müller, K.: Verkehrsarchitektur in der Bundesrepublik Deutschland. Inter Nationes/Moos Verlag, Bonn-Bad Godesberg/Gräfelfing 1980.

Nestler, P., P.M. Bode: Deutsche Kunst seit 1960. Teil 4: Architektur. Bruckmann, Munich 1976.

Sack, M.: Architektur in der ZEIT. Kritiken und Reportagen über Häuser, Städte und Projekte. Mit einer Einführung von H. Klotz. Bucher, Luzern – Frankfurt am Main 1979.

Schöller, P.: Städtepolitik Stadtumbau und Stadterhaltung in der DDR. F. Steiner Verlag, Stuttgart 1986.

Schreiber, M.: Deutsche Architektur nach 1945. Vierzig Jahre Moderne in der Bundesrepublik. With contributions by P.M. Bode et al. Deutsche Verlagsanstalt, Stuttgart 1986.

Schubert, H.: Moderner Museumsbau: Deutschland, Österreich, Schweiz. Deutsche Verlagsanstalt, Stuttgart 1986.

Schwanke, H.-P.: Im Spannungsfeld zwischen Dekoration und Kunst: – "Kunst" am Bau der 50er Jahre. In: Denkmalpflege im Rheinland, No. 3, p. 129–137, 1991.

Solar-Architektur in der Stadt. LOG ID Symposium, 12. und 13. November 1982 in Tübingen. Veranstalter: Verein für Grüne Solararchitektur. Fricke, Frankfurt am Main 1984.

Topfstedt, Th.: Städtebau in der DDR 1955–1971. In: Seemann-Beiträge zur Kunstwissenschaft. VEB E. A. Seemann, Leipzig 1988.

Wieland, D.: Bauen und Bewahren auf dem Lande. In: Schriftenreihe des Deutschen Nationalkomitees für Denkmalschutz, Vol. 7, Kohlhammer, Stuttgart 1985.

Design

Aicher, O.: Die Küche zum Kochen. Callwey, Munich 1982.

Brock, B., H. U. Reck, IDZ Berlin (Ed.): Stilwandel. DuMont, Cologne 1986.

Bürdek, B. E.: Design – Geschichte, Theorie und Praxis der Produktgestaltung, DuMont, Cologne 1991.

Eckstein, H.: Formgebung des Nützlichen. Marginalien zur Geschichte und Theorie des Design. Edition Marzona, Düsseldorf 1985.

form: Zeitschrift für Gestaltung. Seeheim-Jugenheim (4 ed. annually).

Giedion, S.: Die Herrschaft der Mechanisierung. Europäische Verlagsanstalt, Frankfurt am Main 1982.

Haug, W. F.: Kritik der Warenästhetik. Suhrkamp, Frankfurt am Main 1965.

Lindinger, H. (Ed.): Die Moral der Gegenstände. Ernst & Sohn, Berlin 1989.

Meurer, B., H. Vinçon. Industrielle Ästhetik. Anabas, Gießen 1983.

Mukarovsky, J.: Kapitel aus der Ästhetik. Suhrkamp, Frankfurt am Main 1978.

Pevsner, N.: Wegbereiter moderner Formgebung von Morris bis Gropius. DuMont, Cologne 1983.

Selle, G.: Design – Geschichte in Deutschland – Produktkultur als Entwurf und Erfahrung. DuMont, Cologne 1987.

Welsch, W.: Ästhetisches Denken. Reclam, Stuttgart 1991.

Wolfe, T.: Mit dem Bauhaus leben. Syndikat/EVA, Frankfurt am Main 1984.

Film and Television

Adolf-Grimme-Institut (Ed.): Unsere Medien – unsere Republik. Acht Schwerpunkthefte zu den Merkdaten: 1949, 1955, 1962, 1968, 1970, 1976, 1984, 1989, Marl 1989/1990.

Bausch, H.: Rundfunkpolitik nach 1945. 2 vols. dtv, Munich 1980.

Bock, H.-M. (Ed.): Cinegraph. Lexikon zum deutschsprachigen Film. Edition Text + Kritik, Munich 1984 ff.

Claus, W. (Ed.): Medien-Wende. Wende-Medien? Dokumentation des Wandels im DDR-Journalismus Oktober 1989 – Oktober 1990. Vistas, Berlin 1990.

Dost, M., F. Hopf, A. Kluge: Filmwirtschaft in der Bundesrepublik Deutschland und in Europa. Götterdämmerung in Raten. Carl Hanser Verlag, Munich 1973.

Frei, N.: Hörfunk und Fernsehen. In: W. Benz (Ed.): Die Bundesrepublik Deutschland. Vol. 4: Kultur. Fischer, Frankfurt am Main 1989.

Funkhaus, Berlin (Ed.): Radio im Umbruch. Okt. 1989 – Okt. 1990 im Rundfunk der DDR. Darstellungen, Chronik, Dokumentation, Presseresonanz, Berlin 1990.

Hembus, J.: Der deutsche Film kann gar nicht besser sein. Ein Pamphlet von gestern. Eine Abrechnung von heute. Verlag Rogner & Bernhard, Munich 1981.

Holba, H., P. Spiegel: Reclams deutsches Filmlexikon. Reclam, Stuttgart 1984.

Lerg, W. B., R. Steininger (Ed.): Rundfunk und Politik 1923–1973. Rundfunkforschung, Vol. 3. Wissenschaftsverlag Spiess, Berlin 1975.

Müller, H. (Ed.): Film in der BRD. Henschel, Berlin 1990.

Pflaum, H. G.: Deutschland im Film. Themenschwerpunkte des Spielfilms in der Bundesrepublik Deutschland. Max Hueber Verlag, Munich 1985.

Pflaum, H. G.: Germany on Film. Wayne State University Press, Detroit 1990.

Pflaum, H. G., H. H. Prinzler: Film in der Bundesrepublik Deutschland. Der neue deutsche Film. Herkunft/Gegenwärtige Situation. Ein Handbuch. Carl Hanser Verlag, Munich 1979.

Pflaum, H. G., H. H. Prinzler: Film in der Bundesrepublik Deutschland. Der neue deutsche Film. Herkunft/Gegenwärtige Situation. Ein Handbuch, aktualisierte Ausgabe. Inter Nationes, Bonn-Bad Godesberg 1985. (New edition in preparation)

Reimers, K. F., R. Steinmetz (Ed.): Rundfunk in Deutschland. Ölschläger, Munich 1988.

Seidl, C.: Der deutsche Film der fünfziger Jahre. Heyne, Munich 1987.

Steinmetz, R.: Das Studienprogramm des Bayerischen Rundfunks. Entstehung und Entwicklung des Dritten Fernsehprogramms in Bayern 1961–1970. Ölschläger, Munich 1984.

Steinmetz, R.: Freies Fernsehen. Kommerzialisierung und Rundfunkfreiheit im Verständnis der Adenauer Regierungen.

Wehmeier, K.: Die Geschichte des ZDF. Part I: Entstehung und Entwicklung 1961–1966. Hase & Koehler, Mainz 1979.

Customs and Festivals

Alte Bräuche – Frohe Feste. Mairs Geographischer Verlag, Ostfildern 1984.

Bastian, H.: Mummenschanz. Syndikat, Frankfurt am Main 1983.

Fillipetti, H., J. Trotereau: Zauber, Riten und Symbole. Magisches Brauchtum im Volksglauben. Verlag Hermann Bauer, Freiburg im Breisgau 1987.

Kirchhoff, H.: Christliches Brauchtum im Jahreskreis. Kösel, Munich 1990.

Koren, H.: Volksbrauch im Kirchenjahr. Pinguin-Verlag, Innsbruck 1986.

Küster, J.: Bräuche im Kirchenjahr. Herder, Freiburg im Breisgau 1986.

Mezger, W.: Narrenidee und Fastnachtsbrauch. Universitätsverlag, Constance 1991.

Michaelis, H.-Th.: Schützengilden. Keyser, Munich 1985.

Moser, D.-R.: Fastnacht, Fasching, Karneval. Verlag Styria, Cologne 1986.

Raabe, L.: Alte Weihnachtsbräuche aus deutschsprachigen Ländern. Heyne, Munich 1984.

Schönfeldt, S. Gräfin von: Das große Ravensburger Buch der Feste und Bräuche. O. Maier Verlag, Ravensburg 1987.

Schultz, U. (Ed.): Das Fest. C. H. Beck, Munich 1988.

Vossen, R.: Ostereier – Osterbräuche. Christians, Hamburg 1987.

Publications by Inter Nationes

Fohrbeck, C.: Private Kulturförderung in der Bundesrepublik Deutschland. (German, English) Bonn-Bad Godesberg 1989.

Freund, W.: Die Deutsche Kinder- und Jugendliteratur der Gegenwart (German, English, French, Spanish, Polish, Czech, Hungarian, Russian) Bonn-Bad Godesberg 1987/1990.

Führ, Ch.: Schulen und Hochschulen in der Bundesrepublik Deutschland. (German, English, French, Spanish) Bonn-Bad Godesberg 1988. (Beiheft: Zum Bildungswesen in den fünf neuen Bundesländern der Bundesrepublik Deutschland, 1992)

Hierholzer, M.: Kurt Tucholsky 1890–1935. (German, English, French, Spanish) Bonn-Bad Godesberg 1989.

Inter Nationes (Ed.): Aschenputtel. Bonn-Bad Godesberg: (German/English, German/French 1985), (German/Polish, German/Russian 1990).

Inter Nationes (Ed.): Heinrich Böll – Zu seinem Tode. (German, English, French, Spanish) Bonn-Bad Godesberg 1985.

Inter Nationes (Ed.): Joseph Beuys – Zu seinem Tode. (German, English, French, Spanish) Bonn-Bad Godesberg 1986.

Inter Nationes (Ed.): Kunst heute in der Bundesrepublik Deutschland. (German, English, French, Spanish) Bonn-Bad Godesberg 1988.

Kurz, G.: Das große Schauspiel – Deutschland und die Französische Revolution. (German, English, French) Bonn-Bad Godesberg 1988.

Mackensen, L. von: Deutsche Naturforscher und Erfinder aus vier Jahrhunderten. (German, English, French, Spanish) Bonn-Bad Godesberg 1991.

Massow, V. von: Wissenschaft und Wissenschaftsförderung in der Bundesrepublik Deutschland. (German, English, French, Spanish) Bonn-Bad Godesberg 1986.

Neunzig, H. A.: Eine neue europäische Musik – Heinrich Schütz 1585–1672, Georg Friedrich Händel 1685–1759, Johann Sebastian Bach 1685–1750.

(German, English, French, Spanish, Port.) Bonn-Bad Godesberg 1985.

Ruland, J.: Deutsche Weihnachten. (German, English, French, Spanish, Italian) Bonn-Bad Godesberg 1978.

Schoenberner, G. (Ed.): Künstler gegen Hitler. Bonn-Bad Godesberg: (German, English, French, Spanish, Italian) 1984), (Russian, Polish 1991).

Vinke, H.: Carl von Ossietzky 1889–1989. (German, English, French, Spanish) Bonn-Bad Godesberg 1989.

Zimmer, E., R. Köthe: Jugend forscht – Ein Wettbewerb und seine Geschichte in der Bundesrepublik Deutschland (German, English, French, Spanish) Bonn-Bad Godesberg 1986.

Index of Names

Sources of Illustrations

Alexander von Humboldt-Stiftung, Bonn, p. 236; G. Amos, Heidelberg, p. 86 (2); Wolfgang Arnold, Frankfurt am Main, p. 184 (1); Ulrike Bahrs, Munich, p. 133 (1); Basis Filmverleih, Berlin, p. 198 (2); Clärchen Baus-Mattar, Cologne, p. 94 (1); Bavaria Filmstudios, Munich, p. 186 (39; Bavaria Luftbild, Munich, p. 149 (1); Bayreuther Festspiele, Bayreuth, p. 113 (2); Frank Roland Beeneken, Berlin, p. 93 (1); Thilo Beu, Dortmund, p. 91 (1); Adelheid Beyer, Berlin, p. 87 (1); Bildstelle der Stadt Nürnberg, p. 170; BMW, Munich, p. 156; M. Böttcher, Halle, p. 185 (1); Ingrid Brock, Schwarzenbruck, p. 148 (1), 150 (1), 151, 152, 153 (2), 154 (2), 169 (1), 173 (2), 174 (1); Volker Brüggemann, Bad Hersfeld, p. 137; Bundesbildstelle Bonn, p. 67 (1), 130 (2); Rosemarie Clausen, Hamburg, p. 90; Deutsche Presseagentur, dpa, Frankfurt am Main, p. 69 (1), 216 (1), 233 (2); Deutsche Presseagentur, dpa, Munich, p. 45 (1), 222, 223, (2), 225 (2), 226, 227 (2); Deutsche Staatsoper, Berlin, p. 95 (1); Deutsche Stiftung für internationale Entwicklung, Berlin, p. 238; Deutscher Akademischer Austauschdienst, Bonn, p. 242; Carl Duisberg Gesellschaft, Cologne, p. 237; Mara Eggert, Frankfurt am Main, p. 92 (1), 112 (1); Verlag Ellermann, Munich, p. 33; Escada, Dornach, p. 181 (2); Filmverlag der Autoren, Munich, p. 197 (2); Fotoarchiv Bolliger/Ketterer, CH-Campione d'Italia, p. 36 (1); Foto-Bingel, Bad Hersfeld, p. 88 (1); Günter Freyse, Munich, p. 195 (1); Klaus Fröhlich, Freiburg, p. 96 (1); B. Glier et al., Berlin, p. 185 (1); Bernd Peter Goebbels, Hirzenhain, p. 129 (2); Reinhard Görner, Berlin, p. 155 (1) Goethe-Institut, Munich, p. 241 (3); Anneliese Heuer, Berlin, p. 91 (1); Hainer Hill, Berlin, p. 84; Hochschule für Film und Fernsehen, Munich, p. 194 (3), 197 (1), 198 (3); Winfried Hösl, Munich, p. 74 (1); Theo Holtebrinck, Penzberg, p. 139; Rebecca Horn, Munich, p. 50 (2); Institut für Auslandsbeziehungen, Stuttgart, p. 116 (1), 239; Internationales Musikinstitut, Darmstadt, p. 110 (1); Inter Nationes, Bonn, p. 148(1), 155 (1), 157 (1), 181 (1), 184 (2), 243; Jukka Jokilehto, Rome, p. 160 (2); Johannes Klais, Bonn, p. 124; Heinz Köster, Berlin, p. 24 (1); Anka Kröhnke, Hamburg, p. 132; Arwid Lagenpusch, Berlin, p. 94 (1), 95 (1); Landesamt für Denkmalpflege Sachsen, Dresden, p. 160 (1); Landesdenkmalamt Baden-Württemberg, Stuttgart, p. 175; Landesbildstelle Berlin, p. 167; Landeshauptstadt Hannover, p. 169 (1); Landesmuseum Schleswig, Kiel, p. 134 (1); Dagmar Lißke, Greifswald, p. 135; LOG ID/D. Schempp, Tübingen, p. 157 (2); Luchterhand Literaturverlag, Frankfurt am Main, p. 30 (1); Luftbildverlag Bertram, Munich, p. 171 (1); Knut Maron, Essen, p. 97 (1); Mercedes Benz, Stuttgart, p. 182 (1); Messegesellschaft Frankfurt am Main, p. 28 (2); Isgard Moje-Wohlgemuth, Schwanewede, p. 136; Museum für Kunsthandwerk, Frankfurt am Main, p. 138 (1); Museum für Kunst und Gewerbe, Hamburg, p. 138 (1); Museum Ludwig,Cologne, p. 6; Alexander Neumeister, Munich, p. 182 (1); Isolde Ohlbaum, Munich, p. 30 (1); Galerie Pfefferle, Munich, p. 44 (1); Thomas Piltz, Munich, p. 73 (2), 99 (1), 100, 173 (1), 183 (2), 211 (1); Willi Pistor, Hadamar, p. 133 (1); Presse-Bilderdienst Wilhelm Meinberg, Ludwigshafen, p. 68; Rabanus, Munich, p. 85 (1); Edgar Reitz Filmgesellschaft, Munich, p. 207; G. Rohweder, Hamburg, p. 172 (2); Sächsische Landesbibliothek Dresden, p. 72 (1); Jochen Schade, Frankfurt am Main, p. 129 (1); Peter Scharf, Berlin, p. 140 (1); Heinz Spielmann, Hamburg, p. 134 (1); Stadtbildstelle Essen, p. 98 (2); Stadt Dresden, p. 160 (1); Stadt Leipzig, p. 26 (2), 67 (1); Oda Sternberg, Munich, p. 89 (2); Stiftung Deutsche Kinemathek, Berlin, p. 196 (2); Künstlersekretariat Rolf Sudbrack, Hamburg, p. 123 (1); Süddeutscher Verlag, Munich, p. 23 (7), 30/31 (12), 36 (6), 87 (1), 96 (1), 108 (1), 110 (1), 111 (1), 114 (1), 118 (1), 119, 120; Thalia Theater, Hamburg, p. 86 (1); Thyssen AG,

Duisburg, p. 149 (1); United Artists, Frankfurt am Main, p. 194 (1), 195; USIS, Munich, p. 234; Verkehrsamt Köln, p. 70 (3), 71; Ruth Waltz, Berlin, p. 93 (1); Gudrun Webel, Essen, p. 92 (1); Hermann Wehmeyer, Hildesheim, p. 168 (2); ZDF, Mainz, p. 210, 213 (1). All other illustrations from BMS Picture Service.